PR... D0485562

"*Home of the Brave* stirs the deepest p... ... .merican spirit. An inspirational portrait of ordinary Americans doing extraordinary things."

> —W. E. B. Griffin, *New York Times* bestselling author of
> *The Hostage*

"Caspar Weinberger's leadership in rebuilding America's strength to win the Cold War was marked throughout by a fixation on the individual servicemen—not just to arm them, but inspire them, support them, and listen to them. This thrilling book is another of his valuable contributions to honor those heroic men and women."

> —John F. Lehman, former secretary of the navy
> and member of the 9/11 Commission

"*Home of the Brave* tells Americans stories they need to know about the men who are defending our freedom and security. It will leave you breathless at times—and hopeful about our future."

> —Thomas Fleming, *New York Times* bestselling author of
> *Washington's Secret War: The Hidden History of Valley Forge*

"Riveting sagas of extraordinary heroism in combat by members of our armed forces during one of the most difficult, frustrating, and critical conflicts in our history. A must-read for all Americans who care about the future."

> —General P. X. Kelley, USMC (ret.), 28th Commandant
> of the U.S. Marine Corps

AISE FOR HOME OF THE BRAVE

A parts of the A

HOME
of the
BRAVE

HONORING THE UNSUNG HEROES
IN THE WAR ON TERROR

Caspar W. Weinberger
and Wynton C. Hall

 A TOM DOHERTY ASSOCIATES BOOK • New York

NOTE: If you purchased this book without a cover, you should be aware that this book is stolen property. It was reported as "unsold and destroyed" to the publisher, and neither the author nor the publisher has received any payment for this "stripped book."

HOME OF THE BRAVE: HONORING THE UNSUNG HEROES IN THE WAR ON TERROR

Copyright © 2006 by the Estate of Caspar W. Weinberger and by Wynton C. Hall

All rights reserved, including the right to reproduce this book, or portions thereof, in any form.

A Forge Book
Published by Tom Doherty Associates, LLC
175 Fifth Avenue
New York, NY 10010

www.tor-forge.com

Forge® is a registered trademark of Tom Doherty Associates, LLC.

ISBN-13: 978-0-7653-5703-8
ISBN-10: 0-7653-5703-8

First Edition: May 2006
First Mass Market Edition: June 2007

Printed in the United States of America

0 9 8 7 6 5 4 3 2

For the men and women whose love for America
compels them to defend freedom each day

Ours would not be the land of the free if it were not also the home of the brave.

—GEORGE H. W. BUSH

JUNE 1989

CONTENTS

PREFACE   *The Best Among Us*   13

1.   Marine Captain Brian Chontosh   21
     Rochester, New York
     Navy Cross, Iraq

     Marine Corporal Armand McCormick
     Mount Pleasant, Iowa
     Silver Star, Iraq

     Marine Sergeant Robert Kerman
     Klamath Falls, Oregon
     Silver Star, Iraq

2.   Army Sergeant First Class Javier Camacho   39
     Bayamon, Puerto Rico
     New Port Richey, Florida
     Silver Star, Iraq

3.   Marine Sergeant Marco Martínez   49
     Las Cruces, New Mexico
     Navy Cross, Iraq

4.   Air Force Master Sergeant William "Calvin" Markham   67
     Waukesha, Wisconsin
     Silver Star, Afghanistan

5. Army Master Sergeant Patrick Quinn 77
Cromwell, Connecticut
Silver Star, Iraq

6. Marine First Sergeant Justin LeHew 87
Temecula, California
Navy Cross, Iraq

7. Navy Hospital Corpsman Third Class Luis Fonseca, Jr. 111
Fayetteville, North Carolina
Navy Cross, Iraq

8. Army Sergeant Micheaux Sanders 127
Goldsboro, North Carolina
Silver Star, Iraq

9. Army National Guard Sergeant Leigh Ann Hester 139
Bowling Green, Kentucky
Silver Star, Iraq

Army National Guard Specialist Jason Mike
Radcliff, Kentucky
Silver Star, Iraq

Army National Guard Staff Sergeant Timothy Nein
Henryville, Indiana
Silver Star, Iraq

10. Air Force Staff Sergeant Stephen Achey 153
Sumter, South Carolina
Silver Star, Afghanistan

11. Marine Captain Brent Morel   165
McKenzie, Tennessee
Navy Cross, Iraq

Marine Sergeant William Copeland III
Smithfield, Utah
Navy Cross, Iraq

12. Army Lieutenant Colonel Mark Mitchell   179
Milwaukee, Wisconsin
Distinguished Service Cross, Afghanistan

13. Army Sergeant First Class Paul Ray Smith   201
Tampa, Florida
Medal of Honor, Iraq

14. Marine Sergeant Rafael Peralta   219
Tijuana, Mexico
San Diego, CA
*Purple Heart, Nominated for the
Medal of Honor, Iraq*

AFTERWORD   *Have the Mainstream Media Ignored*   233
                   Our Heroes?

ACKNOWLEDGMENTS   249

NOTES   253

INDEX   263

PREFACE:
THE BEST AMONG US

Those who say we're in a time when there are no heroes—
they just don't know where to look.

—RONALD REAGAN, 1981

Every morning, in cities all across the world, 2.4 million Americans wake up, put on a uniform, kiss their loved ones good-bye, and head out the door to defend freedom. In exchange, they ask for nothing: not wealth, not power, not celebrity. When the spotlight is on them, they fidget uncomfortably, as if somehow they have been given undue attention. "I'm no hero," each will tell you. "I was just doing my job."

It's not an act or false humility. They actually believe it. They are not like the rest of us. They are the soldiers, sailors, airmen, and marines of the United States military. They are the best among us.

To them, protecting America is a *privilege*, an *honor*, a solemn duty that has been passed like a torch from their parents and grandparents and great grandparents before them. As First Sergeant Justin LeHew told us, "It's all the crosses in Arlington Cemetery. It's all those GIs who died over there with my dad on Omaha Beach. You want your generation to do America justice just like that one did."

And they are.

We wrote *Home of the Brave* because we believe deeply that this generation *has*, in fact, done America justice by living up to the sterling service and sacrifice of its predecessors. And that's no small feat. Indeed, the lineage of military sacrifice is long and sacred: In World War I, 117,000 Americans were killed; in World War II, 405,000 died; in the Korean War, 36,500 American lives were taken; and in Vietnam, 58,000 patriots were killed.

To the men and women waging the global war against terrorism, these giants upon whose shoulders they stand are not merely statistics. They are beacons, figures whose gallantry illumines their way as they continue the centuries-old task of protecting freedom's future. Perhaps because of the seriousness of their life's calling, today's soldiers, sailors, airmen, and marines are in touch with history in ways most civilians simply are not.

Talk to them. Ask them about their military heritage. Then sit and listen as they recount the names and stories of the American heroes whose example propels them forward, names like: John Basilone, Daniel Daly, Eddie Rickenbacker, Carl Brashear, Edward "Butch" O'Hare, Richard I. Bong, Chester Nimitz, Thomas Kelley, Lewis "Chesty" Puller, Audie Murphy. Most young people today would be hard pressed to identify these individuals. But for those who serve, these ghosts of valor ignite something deep within them. They matter.

And so do the myriad heroes in our midst. Tom Brokaw's fabulous book, *The Greatest Generation*, gave the World War II generation its name. But the current generation of U.S. servicemen and servicewomen also is leaving its own distinct mark on the long history of American service. Unlike the soldiers of World War II, who were drafted, today's military is made up of mothers, fathers, husbands, and wives who volunteered for service. In numbers greater than ever before, reservists also are in harm's way, leaving their civilian jobs for the battlefield. And families are literally in the crossfire. During World War II, parents often were exempt from the draft. In today's military, mothers and fathers in life-threatening situations are common.

Critics, taking their cues from the media, once branded young Americans as overeducated, unmotivated slackers whose greatest day-to-day concern was the speed of their Internet connection. But those who know today's service members best know that such characterizations describe them least. In the War on Terror, the "slackers" have more than held their own when compared with soldiers, sailors, airmen, and marines of past eras.

To most veterans, this comes as little surprise. But the mainstream media aren't communicating that message often enough or even at all. For example, if you asked Americans to identify Britney Spears, Paris Hilton, or Michael Jackson, most could do so correctly. But what if, instead of these three celebrities, citizens were asked to identify Air Force Master Sergeant William "Calvin" Markham or Marine Sergeant Marco Martínez or even Medal of Honor recipient Army Sergeant First Class Paul Ray Smith? Would they be familiar with these individuals? Are *you* familiar with each of these individuals?

Our guess is that you aren't. After all, we weren't. That is, not until we began researching and interviewing several of the individuals whose stories we recount. Does this make us all ungrateful or unpatriotic because we are unfamiliar with the actions of these modern-day American heroes? Of course not. But it does mean that our nation has yet to hear the other side of the story—the side many in the media have refused to tell—about our nation's brave young people fighting in the War on Terror.

It would, of course, be impossible to write about all of the extraordinary members of our armed forces. But the heroism and valor of the nineteen individuals we write about—some of the most highly decorated in the U. S. military—are emblematic of the spirit that pulses through all who have ever worn the uniform. Their jaw-dropping acts of bravery represent but a fraction of the heroic actions that have been performed in the War on Terror. And yet, sadly, most Americans have never even heard their names or those of whose lives they saved.

Their reasons for joining the military are as diverse as the individuals themselves. Some were born into families with long, distinguished histories of military service. Others, however, set a precedent by becoming the first in their family to enlist. For some, the military represented an opportunity to get their lives back on track, to develop discipline, and to sharpen their focus. For others, enlisting in the military meant turning down lucrative career offers in other fields. But they do have one thing in common: a deep and abiding passion for America. The September 11 terrorist attacks galvanized their resolve to wage war against global terrorism.

To be sure, the naysayers and cynics will label that gushing patriotism, sentimental "jingoism." But it's not. Instead, it is the same faithful, steely spirit that rushes through American history and fuels freedom. Like the waves of Americans who came before them, they are not embarrassed about their love for America nor do they hide it, and, as they readily confess, they don't relate well to those who ever would. To them, America *is* worth dying for. And as their stories will reveal, instead of slogans, they have offered service—gritty, dangerous, tenacious service.

They took these actions with the full knowledge that what they did would bring neither fame nor fortune. But when you ask them, they will tell you that's all right. "After all," one hero told us, "that isn't why I joined." He joined for the same reason anyone joins: to be part of something bigger than himself.

This book is also our way of piercing the wall of noise surrounding the War on Terror. Debate is healthy. Indeed, in a representative democracy, it is essential. But when critics begin turning their rhetorical guns on the men and women of our armed forces that's when it is time to say "Enough." The United States is at war, and the enemy we face is as dangerous and determined as any in our nation's history. Although they will never seek our praise or accolades, the 2.4 million members of our armed forces deserve our prayers, support, and gratitude. They've more than earned it.

Finally, having the privilege to get to know many of the individuals whose stories we recount and to learn about their experiences has been one of the great honors of our careers. In sharing their stories, we hope that Americans will reaffirm their appreciation and commitment to the men and women who, like the generations of American warriors before them, stand ready to do violence on our behalf.

America did not start this War on Terror, but we will win it. And when we do, we will have them—the best among us—to thank for it. Let us not wait until then to begin expressing our gratitude.

HOME
of the
BRAVE

1

Marine Captain Brian Chontosh
NAVY CROSS

Marine Corporal Armand McCormick
SILVER STAR

Marine Sergeant Robert Kerman
SILVER STAR

IRAQ

I'm very optimistic. It's awesome. It's beautiful. We're watching what America looked like right from the get-go that we weren't around to see over two hundred years ago. All the challenges and everything—they're not going to be perfect in a day. It took us two hundred years to get it halfway right.

—CAPTAIN BRIAN CHONTOSH

Two words. That was all it took.

"Push forward!" Captain Brian Chontosh yelled.

Like the swipe of a match across the strike plate, the marine captain's words ignited actions that would forever change the lives of five men. They would be outnumbered almost thirty to one. They would find themselves closer to death than at any other time in their lives, forcing them to put their fate into each others' hands. But above all, they would learn that in war, just as in life, sometimes the only way through danger is to "push forward."

That was certainly the case March 25, 2003, when then-Lieutenant Brian R. Chontosh, thirty-one, served as leader of his Combined Anti-Armor Team platoon (CAAT) for Third Battalion, Fifth Marine Regiment, First Marine Division, First Marine Expeditionary Force. Six feet tall and two hundred pounds, with chiseled facial features, the Rochester, New York, native is no stranger to peril. His mother, Robin Chontosh, says she sensed her son's courage early on.

"He's always been fearless," said his mother. "We always called him our wild child."[1]

Long before Captain Chontosh put on a marine uniform, he had dreams of wearing a different uniform entirely. "I went to college to play baseball," he told us. "I thought I was going to be a major league baseball star. I was a middle infielder. I wasn't that good, but every kid's got that dream."

His short stint playing college ball had been the culminating event in eighteen years of a life that, according to him, lacked direction, focus, and discipline. "I owe who I am today as a man to the military." Although not born into a "military family," the New Yorker says it was the tradition and mystique surrounding the Marine Corps that drew him in.

"I'm part of something greater than myself—a brotherhood, a bond. You read the stories of the guys who've gone before us, and I can't even hope to hold up the weight half as much as they did. You have that sense of tradition. I always told my men I wanted to be a 'dude among dudes.' I love the camaraderie, the companionship. It's addictive to me and very, very rewarding to see people grow as human beings."

Baseball teams consist of nine players, but that blistering day in Ad Diwaniyah, Iraq, Captain Chontosh's team consisted of only four other men, all of whom he would soon see flourish. One of these individuals was Corporal Armand McCormick. The two men have known each other for over three years. They are, in many ways, different: Chontosh grew up in Rochester, New York, with close to a quarter of a million people. McCormick, on the other hand, hails from the quiet town of Mount Pleasant, Iowa, population nine thousand. Despite their different upbringings, McCormick, twenty-three, says one word best explains the bond between them: *mentality*.

"I knew as soon as stuff happened that we were going to go into it. That's just the kind of person he [Chontosh] is. That's why he and I got along so well. I knew it would happen. The whole time we were there we would just do fun stuff like that. His leadership goes above and beyond," said McCormick.

Joining in Captain Chontosh and Corporal McCormick's "fun" would be a relative latecomer to the platoon, then-Lance Corporal Robert "Robbie" Kerman. It was the terrorist attacks on September 11, 2001, that had propelled Kerman into the Marine Corps. "He was a freshman at University of Nevada, Reno, when 9/11 happened," Kerman's father recalls. "He called me September 12 and said, 'I want to quit school and do something meaningful. I want to join the corps.'" Kerman's father could hardly protest his son's decision: "I did the same thing in 1966, when I was a freshman at UCLA and Vietnam was raging."[2]

"Kerman came fresh out of school," said Chontosh. "Young kid. His father was in Third Battalion, Fifth Marines in Vietnam, and he wanted to go serve in the same unit his father had served in. We took him under our wing. He came to the platoon real late and was one of the last ones to come into our platoon. He got meritoriously promoted that day to sergeant. Kerman is fabulous!"

As it happened, 9/11 had similarly galvanized Captain Chontosh's determination: "I'd just got done from a PT run. The guys were like, 'Sir, you've got to check this out.' I got there just as the second plane was hitting. I couldn't believe it. I sat there with the same shock as everyone else. . . . I remember having this one thought: I am so lucky right now to be me, because I'm going to be able to do something for my country. I'm going to have a chance to do something about this."

When his chance finally came, Chontosh's five-man Humvee team included two more members, Corporal Thomas "Tank" Franklin, a .50-caliber machine gunner by specialty, and Corporal Korte, their Humvee radio operator.

"Thomas 'Tank' Franklin? Oh man! Tom Franklin is the best machine gunner with the .50-cal I've ever come across," said Captain Chontosh. "This is Thomas Franklin who is on terminal leave—he's out of the Marine Corps—and is going to college at Florida. Stop loss date was put into effect, and he'd made the cutoff date by four or five days; he could have stayed on terminal leave. He was my driver all the way through training, and he's a damn good .50-cal gunner. So I picked up the phone and said, 'Frankie, I gotta have you back, man.' He said, 'Are you serious?' I said, 'Yeah, we're leaving in about a week. He said, 'I'm on my way.' I had called in the middle of his math class, and he walked out of class, went home to his wife, and said, 'Honey, I've got to go.' So he got on a bird and flew back."

Brian Chontosh might have traded the baseball diamond for the battlefield, but he had a new team, one comprised of corporals McCormick, Kerman, Franklin, and Korte. And he says he wouldn't have had it any other way. On March 25, 2003, he would lead these men headlong into danger so that their marine brothers wouldn't have to.

Captain Chontosh, known to his men as "Big Fish" or "Tosh," didn't like the looks of the eight-foot-tall berm lining the sides of Highway 1, just outside Baghdad, south of Ad Diwaniyah. The terrain was mostly desert, with small vegetation just beginning to spring up through the sandy soil. The roughly eighty-man platoon had been at war for five days now and had seen minimal action. But Chontosh knew that could and would change at a moment's notice.

The column was led by four M1-A1 Abrams tanks, which were followed by seven thin-skinned Humvees, each with a .50-caliber machine gun turret on top. Then-Lieutenant Chontosh rode in the passenger's seat. His vehicle was the first of the Humvees and trailed the last of the Abrams tanks by about fifty meters. McCormick was driving, Corporals Franklin and Kerman were at the turret, and Korte was at the radio. The arrangement was somewhat atypical. Having traveled hundreds of miles and not seen much action, the marines had become bored and thought it might be fun to break the monotony by shuffling their usual roles. McCormick, a basic rifleman, had never driven the Humvee.

"It's a little after five A.M. Iraq time, and it's starting to look like it's going to be another boring day," remembers Corporal McCormick. "But we only make it about two kilometers. We see some action up in front of the tanks: a white civilian truck—it looked like it had people in back. That's when we came up on the man-made berm. It's pretty tall, twenty-five meters off the road, and about eight feet tall. Captain Chontosh looks over and says, 'I'm a little nervous about that berm.' So he radios to the rest of our trucks to keep an eye out on this berm and that it looks a little suspicious."

The M1-A1 Abrams tanks in front of their Humvee (call sign "Blue One") came to an abrupt halt. McCormick mashed the break pedal.

Huge flashes streaked through the air in front of them. They were rocket-propelled grenades (RPG). The tanks stopped and buttoned up—the gunner quickly ducked inside and the vehicle commander scurried inside—but the tanks weren't moving. They just sat there.

"Push forward, Blue One! Push, push, push!" yelled Captain Chontosh.

Mortars, small-arms fire, and RPGs began flooding the kill zone. With the tanks blocking the thin-skinned Humvees, Chontosh's vehicle and the others were now stationary targets; they were trapped. The tanks started to inch forward, only to jerk in fits and starts. Corporal McCormick was itching to grab his M-16, dismount the vehicle, and "do some damage." He was a rifleman by specialty. Instead of his weapon, however, his hands were now gripped around the steering wheel of their Humvee.

Chontosh's eyes darted back and forth across Highway 1.

He couldn't see where the fire was coming from. No one could. The berm had obstructed their view. But he was determined to find the source of the enemy fire. He ordered Mc-Cormick to whip out of the column and off-road the vehicle.

"I have no idea what was going on at that time. I don't want to say it was instinct. I don't want to say it was training. It all boils down to luck and chance I think. Just aggressive action. We just had to do something. I want to say that my mind was perfectly clear, but I wasn't thinking," said Chontosh.

He then spotted a small "driveway" that led into the berm. Covering from vegetation almost prevented the marines from catching the tiny entryway. McCormick was driving fast. He jerked a hard right. The Humvee barely fit through the snug driveway. It felt like he was driving through a narrow hallway.

"As soon as we take a right, we see this machine-gun bunker. We see just flashes shooting at us. Corporal Franklin sitting on top with the .50-cal just neutralizes that bunker within seconds—right away," said McCormick.

The decision to have Franklin on the .50-caliber had proved fateful. He was an ace on the gun and could shoot with devastating accuracy, even while moving at high speeds. Had Franklin not locked in on the five Iraqis blasting away from their machine-gun bunker, the five marines might have been killed the instant their Humvee penetrated the berm.

The sight was something to behold, even for the seasoned Chontosh: "Franklin's free-gunning with the .50-cal off road and shooting accurately while we're on the move. It was amazing to watch."

Equally adept were McCormick's driving skills. He floored the Humvee while averting enemy fire before whipping the vehicle into a tight indentation in the berm that served as a makeshift "parking spot." The area inside the enemy nest was large, about two hundred meters or so in size. A trench lay just across the way. Chontosh, Kerman, and McCormick leapt out of the vehicle. Franklin stayed on the .50-caliber, Korte on the radio.

"I jumped out," said McCormick. "Franklin asked me for a can of ammo. 'Tosh' and Kerman are running down into the trench. I caught up to them and ran in there too. We ran almost two hundred yards. That's when all hell breaks loose. There were guys everywhere. I was just shooting. There were enemy everywhere. There were people five feet in front of us. We had to run by and double tap to make sure they were gone as we made our way down the trench. . . . I holstered my 9 mm and grabbed an AK-47 that was laying on the ground. But the enemy were on top of us. Just right there, right on us. There was nothing to duck behind," McCormick recalls.

Entering the trench had been the equivalent of a boot stomping on an ant mound. The minute the three marines entered the trench, enemy fighters flooded the zone. Official estimates indicated that the three marines had been swarmed by a company-sized element of roughly 150 to 200 Iraqi fighters. The deafening noise emanating from Corporal Franklin's .50-caliber machine gun had sent many of the enemy soldiers scrambling for cover. But the fiercest Iraqis were now engaging the three young marines in groups of five and six in close-quarter combat, often at an arm's-length distance.

Always quick to share credit with his boys, Chontosh says it was Kerman and McCormick's skills that kept him alive. "They saved my life that day without a doubt. Kerman the way he's shootin'; McCormick the way he's driving. Kerman was so cool: just one shot, one shot, one shot. He was so cool in there," said Chontosh.

What the gracious leader fails to mention, however, was that as Kerman and McCormick were shooting with the utmost proficiency, Captain Chontosh was busy taking down at least twenty enemy shooters with his M-16 rifle and 9 mm pistol. Some of the enemy fighters wore civilian rags; others donned war belts. But each Iraqi had been outfitted with an impressive array of AK-47s, 9 mm pistols, and RPG launchers. As the three marines dropped enemy after enemy, weapons of opportunity began multiplying on the battlefield.

"I grabbed an AK-47 and just let it fly," said Chontosh.

Asked what he was thinking during the close-quarter combat assault, Corporal McCormick responded, "I was thinking, 'I need some more ammo!' That's what I'm thinking!"

Kerman, the new guy, the "boot" as marines call them, was rapidly gaining respect in the hearts and minds of the other four. His calm, sure demeanor and skillful shooting elevated his status instantly.

Even though the first flurry of action inside the trench had now begun to calm slightly, the rest of the platoon still had no clue about the brutal battle their five marine brothers were caught in. There had been no time for Chontosh to establish communication with the tanks. Meanwhile, Corporal Korte, the radio operator, had cautioned the rest of the platoon about entering the trench. Doing so, he worried, might increase the odds of a possible friendly fire tragedy.

Still, Chontosh, McCormick, and Kerman had to somehow make it back to Franklin and Korte, who were waiting in the truck. Two football fields' worth of distance separated them from their Humvee. With Iraqis still firing at them, they decided to make a run for it and dashed through the trench toward their vehicle. Along the way, Corporal McCormick had snatched up an enemy RPG launcher and tossed it to Chontosh.

"If you can figure out how to fire this thing, we can get the hell out of here," McCormick said.

Captain Chontosh quickly looked the weapon over. He then raised it into a firing position before squeezing the trigger. A grenade shot out of the weapon and skimmed across the ground, sending enemy fighters scurrying for cover. The act of turning the enemy fighters' own weapon against them bought McCormick enough time to get back behind the wheel.

"Going out of there I was going as fast as a Humvee can drive," McCormick said.

When the dust settled, Chontosh had cleared two hundred meters of enemy trench, killed more than twenty Iraqi fighters, and wounded numerous others. But when their Humvee broke through the berm and back out onto Highway 1, there was no time for Chontosh or his teammates to contemplate the gravity of the events that had just unfolded. Indeed, as the day turned to night, McCormick realized he had almost forgotten the significance of the date: It was his twenty-first birthday.

"There was absolutely no time to think of anything about what had happened," said Chontosh. "Immediately after that action, tanks were on the radio calling for infantry support. There's no time to think about dying. I was more scared two or three days after it was all over. It didn't hit me until after the fact. I was more scared after the fact than I ever was during the action."

That night the men of Third Battalion, Fifth Marines had other things on their minds. A horrendous sandstorm had sent blinding waves of sand crashing against their vehicles. There was so much sand whooshing through the air that not even their night-vision goggles (NVG) and thermal imaging worked. Captain Chontosh and Corporal McCormick were exhausted from the hell they had experienced inside the enemy trench, but they refused to sleep that night. Instead, the two men rode vehicle to vehicle checking on their platoon's general welfare and morale. Platoon Leader Chontosh's primary concern remained his boys, many of whom had just experienced their first taste of battle.

"When it all calmed down we all started laughing about how crazy it was," said McCormick. "We started talking about what all happened in there and what in the hell we were thinking. Franklin kept asking questions and telling us we were crazy. During the deal, there was really no thinking. Afterwards we laughed about it. It was pretty funny that I took that RPG and had 'Tosh' shoot it. That's kind of a no-no to mess around with foreign weapons."

But Chontosh realized that extreme circumstances sometimes demand extreme action. As it happened, the danger they had encountered that day would be a harbinger of things to come. In the days that followed, action picked up dramatically. While there would be no more close-quarter battles that rivaled the intensity of those of March 25, Chontosh and his men took fire virtually every day thereafter.

On May 6, 2004, at a ceremony at Marine Corps Air Ground Combat Training Center, Twentynine Palms, California, the commandant of the U.S. Marine Corps, General Michael W. Hagee, awarded the second-highest award a marine can receive, the Navy Cross, to Captain Chontosh. The third-highest award, the Silver Star, went to Corporals Armand McCormick and Robert Kerman. "They are the reflection of the Marine Corps type whose service to the Marine Corps and country is held above their own safety and lives," said General Hagee.

Captain Chontosh's wife, Joy, and their two children, Sara and Colby, know the truth behind General Hagee's words all too well. "She [Joy Chontosh] gets nervous and goes through some emotional times," said Captain Chontosh. "I'm pretty fortunate, though. She's been through a lot. She's been through three deployments in four years. Two combat tours. Knowing that she's as strong as she is allows me to go away and focus on my job. She's been phenomenal."

The ceremony and accolades meant a lot to Captain Chontosh, but they're not what he cherishes most. "You don't need to get rewarded. I've got something between me and Armand, Robbie Kerman, Franklin, all those guys, the whole platoon. We've got something close. We've got something we can share," Chontosh told us.

Corporal Kerman, twenty-one, a Klamath Falls, Oregon, native, had not only earned the respect of his new platoon, he had also lived up to the fine tradition of his father's service as a marine in Third Battalion, Fifth Marines. "I was pretty scared at the time, but we knew what we had to do and we did it," Kerman said. "I did not expect the award. Maybe I just did the right thing."[3]

As for Corporal McCormick, immediately following the ceremony he had some important business to tend to. The

May 6 awards ceremony was to mark his discharge from the marines, but McCormick had just received word that his buddies weren't getting out until sometime in September or October as combat replacements. "So I walked over and did some work on the extension papers to go back for another three months. I left the day after I got the Silver Star to go back to Iraq. I didn't want to see my buddies go to war while I was home relaxing and enjoying life, all the while knowing they were over there in danger." McCormick's fiancée, Lacey Meyers, wasn't wild about her future husband's decision to voluntarily hop on a plane and head back to the battlefield within twenty-four hours, but she respected it. Deeply.

Today, Armand McCormick is a full-time criminology major at the University of Northern Iowa. Having spent seven months fighting during Operation Iraqi Freedom, the former marine says he misses the corps more than he ever imagined. McCormick says the liberal climate that pervades college campuses today combined with the liberal news media has radically distorted the views of many of today's young people: "I've had a few conversations about [the War on Terror] in the liberal classrooms I go to every day. A lot of the time I just look at them and tell them that they don't have any clue what they're talking about, because all they do is listen to liberal news. I always tell them, 'If you don't experience something, how in the hell can you say what will happen?'

"I had a personal experience. Most college campuses, ninety percent of the students are liberals. It was a rainy day and I was walking out of class, and there was this antiwar rally going on. I didn't respond very well. My fiancée and I kind of got into it with all of them. One guy told me, 'If you

think the war is okay, then why don't you go and serve!' . . .
He said, 'The Iraqis don't want us there!' So I asked him,
'How do you know?' A bunch of people got on me and my fi-
ancée's side. We ended up breaking up their rally."

Similarly, Captain Chontosh, who also later fought hero-
ically in Fallujah, Iraq, believes the mainstream media continue to give Americans a stunningly distorted and negative
view that stands in sharp contrast to the countless positive
developments he has seen firsthand:

> Absolutely there's a difference! We're so focused on the nega-
> tive things. I've seen the great, beautiful things. I look at the
> Iraqi children. They're fabulous. . . . The elderly people, when
> you sit and talk to them, you find that they're good, decent,
> people who want us there. . . . There are a lot of great things
> going on there. We talked about the elections, but even in the
> area I was in, Ad Diwuniyah, alone, we built 134 schools!
> Where is that in the news? We refitted two hospitals; clean wa-
> ter is in greater supply than prewar levels; sewage disposal;
> waste management is getting taken care of properly. There are
> a lot of things going on that people don't see and don't want to
> concentrate on. It's not interesting. It's not sexy.

Captain Chontosh says he has learned to not allow the critics and naysayers to stir up negative emotions within him. Instead, he just "lets it go" and remains hopeful about the seeds
of liberation the U.S. military has sown.

"I'm very optimistic," Chontosh told us. "It's awesome. It's
beautiful. We're watching what America looked like right
from the get-go that we weren't around to see over two hun-

dred years ago. All the challenges and everything—they're not going to be perfect in a day. It took us two hundred years to get it halfway right, because we're only halfway right as it is. But it is beautiful to sit and watch it. . . . All I know is that there is a lot of good that we're doing over there that you don't see. The children—we're doing good things."

The children—they stand out in Corporal McCormick's mind as well. He says that at least 80 percent of the Iraqi people "love you, they're all about you. They want you to be here. They're real thankful for you." It's the memory of the children that gives him hope for the future. "There were always these kids sitting outside of our camp," McCormick recalls. "They'd always want to hang out with us. So we would often go play soccer with them. We'd put little security gates out. And someone would go get a soccer ball, and we'd play soccer with the Iraqi kids. They were pretty good, too! They could kick a soccer ball and run around with bare feet. It was fun."

Equally exciting, says McCormick, was the sight of Iraqis voting free in open, democratic elections. "It makes you feel like you've actually accomplished something personally. . . . Deep down inside, there's not anyone who can honestly say that they don't feel as though they've accomplished something over there. I watch the news—FOX News—all the time. I like seeing all the Iraqis so happy. Seeing the women out there voting was awesome! When we were over there, I couldn't believe how the men would walk twenty feet in front of the women, and the women would be carrying all the groceries and the kids. It's awesome now knowing they have some kind of life now. It's a good feeling."

As for Captain Chontosh, the kid from Rochester, New

York, he still exudes the same humility and graciousness that he did before receiving the Navy Cross. "I'm the same person as I was before," Chontosh said. "I'm just an average Joe. There's no hero about it. I was lucky enough to have the day to show what I was capable of doing."

In the end, Captain Chontosh and Corporals Armand McCormick and Robert Kerman say they do not consider themselves heroes, just men that were doing their job, marines that "pressed forward" in the face of certain danger.

OFFICIAL NAVY CROSS CITATION

The President of the United States
takes pleasure in presenting
the Navy Cross
to

Brian Chontosh
United States Marine Corps

for service as set forth in the following:

For extraordinary heroism as Combined Anti-Armor Platoon Commander, Weapons Company, 3rd Battalion, 5th Marines, 1st Marine Division, I Marine Expeditionary Force in support of Operation IRAQI FREEDOM on 25 March 2003. While leading his platoon north on Highway I toward Ad Diwaniyah, First Lieutenant Chontosh's platoon moved into a coordinated ambush of mortars, rocket propelled grenades, and automatic weapons fire. With coalition tanks blocking the road ahead, he realized his platoon was caught in a kill zone. He had his driver move the vehicle through a breach along his flank, where he was immediately taken under fire from an entrenched machine gun. Without hesitation, First Lieutenant Chontosh ordered the driver to advance directly at the enemy position enabling his .50 caliber machine gunner to silence the enemy. He then directed his driver into the enemy trench where he exited his vehicle and began to clear the trench with an M16A2 service rifle and 9 millimeter pistol. His ammunition depleted, First Lieutenant Chontosh, with complete disregard for his safety, twice picked up discarded enemy rifles and continued his ferocious attack. When a Marine following him found an enemy rocket propelled grenade launcher, First Lieutenant Chontosh used it to destroy yet another group of enemy soldiers. When his audacious attack ended, he had cleared over 200 meters of the enemy trench, killing more than 20 enemy soldiers and wounding several others. By his outstanding display of decisive leadership, unlimited courage in the face of heavy enemy fire, and utmost devotion to duty, First Lieutenant Chontosh reflected great credit upon himself and upheld the highest traditions of the Marine Corps and the United States Naval Service.

2

Army Sergeant First Class Javier Camacho
SILVER STAR

★

IRAQ

> It is my hope that some day Adam will have a son who will
> shake Sergeant Camacho's hand and show him that what he
> did was so much more than just his job that day.[1]
> **—MARY KENNEDY, MOTHER OF PRIVATE FIRST CLASS ADAM SMALL,**
> **WHOM SERGEANT CAMACHO SAVED**

Had Sergeant First Class Javier Camacho strictly followed
Army protocol, Mary Kennedy's son, Private First Class
Adam Small, would surely have died. But Camacho, a native
of Bayamon, Puerto Rico, had always been a bit of a maver-
ick. Indeed, residents of Bayamon are often called *vaqueros*
(cowboys). And it was this cowboy spirit that would cement
Sergeant Camacho's hero status in Mary Kennedy's heart and
mind forever.

On March 25, 2003, Private First Class Small sat trapped inside the claustrophobic confines of his flaming Bradley fighting
vehicle when the vehicle's ammunitions, once intended for
Iraqi enemy forces, started to explode. Enemy rocket-propelled

grenades (RPGs) had hit Small's armored vehicle during an ambush on American forces traveling a hundred miles south of Baghdad near the city of Najaf. In an instant, Small's mind flashed to memories of his hometown of Leslie, Michigan.

"As Adam sat there, trapped, with fire and the munitions exploding, he was sure his life was about to end. I'm thankful Sergeant Camacho and God had other plans for him," said Mary Kennedy.[2]

Adam Small had just graduated from high school when he decided to join the army in July 2001, twenty days shy of his eighteenth birthday. Now far removed from the familiar comforts of home, Small scrambled to remember the skills he had learned during boot camp. Still, no amount of knowledge could have trained him to free himself from his burning tank; his escape hatch had jammed shut. As the tank's weaponry caught fire and began to detonate, Private First Class Small was fully aware of the combustible nature of the Bradley's fuel load, his body was rocked with each successive blast. The twenty-one-year-old started to hyperventilate.

This was the crisis Sergeant First Class Javier Camacho, the thirty-five-year-old leader of B Troop, 3/7 Cavalry, decided to enter that fateful day in March. He would follow the Soldier's Creed to never leave a fallen soldier. And although he had never met Mary Kennedy (or her son for that matter), before it was all over, the two individuals would exchange gifts; gifts, each one says, they will cherish for a lifetime. Camacho would give Kennedy her son's life. Mary Kennedy would give Sergeant Camacho a letter. And neither would ever be the same.

That the fighting surrounding Najaf proved to be some of

the fiercest at that time had surprised no one. Considered one of the holiest cities in the Islamic world, Najaf is home to the tomb of Ali, son-in-law and cousin of Mohammed. Fighters in the area included some of Saddam's fiercest and most loyal supporters. In fact, the war waged in Najaf produced the most intense fighting up to that point in Operation Iraqi Freedom.

Adam Small and the other members of the Third Infantry Division were called to the region to capture a bridge. While all involved were well aware of the mission's danger, less predictable were the sandstorms, which were capable of hurling sheets of desert debris against troop movements without warning. The loss of visibility during such episodes was especially dangerous; stationary troops created targets of opportunity for Iraqi attackers lying in wait.

As night fell, Small's group was traveling in front of Sergeant Camacho's, both moving southeast of Najaf, when the column of tanks got caught in a whirlwind of sand. Sensing an opportunity to attack, Iraqi paramilitary troops launched grenades against the U.S. forces, landing direct hits on two Bradleys. Enemy Jeeps mounted with antitank weaponry, along with dismounted infantrymen, flooded the ambush zone. The element of surprise was now on the Iraqis' side. A chaotic fighting environment quickly developed, leaving conditions ripe for incidents of friendly fire. The only natural illumination came from the vehicles' detonating weapons, creating bursts of orange and yellow light.

While his three crewmembers managed to escape the vehicle, Private Small remained trapped in the driver's compartment. He pounded frantically against the escape hatch. As the other men crawled from the tank's turret, they inhaled the poisonous fumes billowing from the explosions, leaving them all too weak to save the vehicle's driver. But among soldiers, no sin is greater than abandoning a fellow comrade in battle. So one of the men, Sergeant Charles Kilgore, signaled to Sergeant Camacho that Private First Class Small remained trapped in the flaming Bradley.

"When they told me he [Small] was still there, my heart stopped," Camacho recalls. He said he remembers thinking, "He's not one of my soldiers, but I could just imagine burning to death in a tank. I wouldn't leave nobody like that."[3] And he didn't.

With the help of Sergeant Jeremiah Gallegos and Sergeant First Class Steven Newby, Camacho led a rescue attempt to retrieve Small, who was, for all intents and purposes, trapped inside a flaming vault. To be successful, Camacho would have to find a way to dodge mortar and gunfire, extinguish the flames surrounding the escape hatch, pry the jammed lid open while dodging gunfire, assist the trapped soldier to safety, and achieve all of these objectives before the tank's weapons and fuel tank incinerated the vehicle and its trapped passenger.

"I crawled as slow as I could, 'cause the tank was still blowing up and rounds were going everywhere," Camacho remembers. "All you could hear was the sound of bullets going by."[4]

As bullets ripped through the darkened Najaf sky, Sergeant Camacho suppressed enemy fire while inching closer to Small's burning tank. Camacho and his men were able to douse the flames that covered the hatch before muscling the door open. Upon lifting the tank's metal cap, the once muffled sound of gunfire ricocheting off targets now filled Adam Small's ears. Reaching into the tank's driver compartment, Javier Camacho met Adam Small for the first time. There would be little conversation between the two soldiers; the twenty-one-year-old Small lay heaving breathlessly. But Adam Small would never forget the name Javier Camacho, a name that his mother, Mary Kennedy, lifts up in her prayers to this day.

After yanking Small out of his flame-covered vehicle, Camacho carried the soldier off the road to a nearby ditch. Sergeant Javier Camacho had just saved Adam Small's life, but heroes seldom think in such terms; the speed of battle doesn't allow it. There was much work yet to be done.

Only eight days after his gallantry in Najaf, Sergeant Camacho was called into action again. This time, he and his men had seen a scout vehicle take fire before bursting into flames. The scene looked eerily familiar. As with Private Small's Bradley fighting vehicle, Iraqi small-arms and rocket-propelled grenade fire had scored a direct hit, leaving American soldiers trapped inside the burning scout transport. This time, however, Camacho decided to use his vehicle as a barrier. By positioning himself between the injured American forces and their Iraqi attackers, Camacho was able to shield American troops from oncoming gunfire before evacuating the wounded soldiers to safety. One of his men, Sergeant Gallegos, says he had no trouble following his leader's call.

"If I could choose to be with anybody, I'd choose to be with him [Sergeant Camacho]. I felt the safest around him."[5]

With the members of the scout vehicle out of harm's way,

Camacho directed his men to finish the job. The soldiers destroyed the enemy forces and secured the area. Army reports indicate that during Operation Iraqi Freedom, the 3/7 Cavalry Division, of which Sergeant Camacho was a member, destroyed 60 Iraqi tanks and killed over 2,200 enemy soldiers on their march toward Baghdad. What these numbers don't reflect, however, is the number of lives—Iraqi and American—these men saved, lives like that of Private Adam Small.

On October 24, 2003, Sergeant First Class Javier Camacho attended a ceremony at Fort Stewart's battalion headquarters, where he was awarded the army's third-highest military honor, the Silver Star. His former wife, Colleen Clark, made the trip up from New Port Richey, Florida, so Camacho's eleven-year-old son, Tyler, could hear his father's superiors declare his dad a hero.

As Battalion Commander Lieutenant Colonel Andrew Fowler and Assistant Division Commander Brigadier General José D. Riojas spoke during the ceremony, both cited Sergeant Camacho as a model soldier, a warrior's warrior.

"Camacho truly embodies the warrior ethos," said Riojas. "He did what he felt was right in his heart and relied on his training and instincts to accomplish the mission."[6]

Lieutenant Colonel Fowler agreed: "I thank Sergeant First Class Camacho for demonstrating what a soldier should truly be."

Camacho, however, remained unimpressed with his actions, even making light of his own valor. "To me, I was just doing my job as an NCO [noncommissioned officer]," Camacho said. "Afterward, I thought it was pretty stupid to have climbed on a burning and exploding tank. It's something we're taught not to do, but I'm glad I did."[7]

Equally grateful was Mary Kennedy. She decided to express her feelings for her son's rescuer in a letter. In it, she told Camacho of her unending gratitude for him and his men. She also wanted Camacho to know she prays for him.

"I told him that I thanked God for him," Kennedy said.[8]

At the end of her missive, she included her home phone number and asked Sergeant Camacho to call her so she could thank him once again for saving her son. She wanted to hear his voice, for him to hear hers.

Sergeant Camacho made that call. He had something he wanted to tell Mary Kennedy, as well. For all the adulation and praise and honors he had received, Camacho wanted Private Small's mother to know that his most treasured memento was the letter she had written thanking him for saving her son's life.

"He said the letter I wrote meant more to him than any medal the army could give him," said Kennedy.[9]

In the most frantic moment in Adam Small's twenty-one-year-old life, Sergeant Javier Camacho—the Vaquero—had followed his gut and remained true to the values of the Soldier's Creed: "I will never leave a fallen comrade." He didn't know who Adam Small was or even that he was Mary Kennedy's son; it didn't matter. All he knew was that one of his own was trapped in a burning vehicle and he had a chance, improbable though it may have been, to do something about it.

As for Mary Kennedy, she has but one final wish: "It is my hope that some day Adam will have a son who will shake

Sergeant Camacho's hand and show him that what he did was so much more than just his job that day. Then maybe Sergeant Camacho will begin to grasp the magnitude of his courage and the depth of our appreciation."[10]

THE SOLDIER'S CREED

I am an American Soldier.

I am a Warrior and a member of a team. I serve the people of the
United States and live the Army Values.

I will always place the mission first.

I will never accept defeat.

I will never quit.

I will never leave a fallen comrade.

I am disciplined, physically and mentally tough, trained and
proficient in my warrior tasks and drills. I always maintain my
arms, my equipment and myself.

I am an expert and I am a professional.

I stand ready to deploy, engage, and destroy the enemies of the
United States of America in close combat.

I am a guardian of freedom and the American way of life.

I am an American Soldier.

3

Marine Sergeant Marco Martínez
NAVY CROSS

★

IRAQ

> I told my mother before I left that if I die not to be upset, be-
> cause I'm not upset. I told her, 'I'll be buried with all my broth-
> ers in arms in Arlington.' She started crying when I said it.
>
> —SERGEANT MARCO MARTÍNEZ

On the night of his high school senior prom, Marco Martínez was nowhere to be found. Try as they might, Martínez's friends couldn't find him anywhere. That is until they piled into their limousine and made their way along the dark streets of Las Cruces, New Mexico, the town where he and his friends lived. As the teens zoomed down the road, they saw the silhouette of a young man jogging alongside the street. It was Martínez. Instead of a tuxedo or suit, the future marine wore shorts, a T-shirt, and running shoes. One of his friends rolled down the car window before yelling "You're crazy, Marco! Loser!"

Undeterred, the young man simply smiled and waved before refocusing on the six miles of road that lay before him.

Martínez had a dream to pursue, one he'd had since the sixth grade. Having signed his Marine Corps papers at age seventeen, this son of a former U.S. Army Ranger wanted to be ready for the thirteen hellish weeks of training that awaited him in San Diego, just one week after his high school graduation.

"My entire senior year of high school, being a marine is all I thought about," Martínez told us. "Being a marine is first and foremost about serving the country. To me, a marine is willing to die for the United States at any given moment, at any given time. They are the first ones to go in and the last ones to come out. That was one of the things that attracted me, because I knew that were I to join I would definitely see some action."

Having grown up listening to his father tell stories about all the action he had experienced as an army Ranger working on counter drug operations in South America, Marco eagerly followed in his father's footsteps. But he says his father never pressured him to pursue his path to join the army; rather, he wanted his son to chart his own course, to have his *own* stories to tell.

On April 12, 2003, during the battle of Tarmiya in Iraq, then Corporal Martínez experienced the most intense four and a half hours of his life. Marco Martínez's actions that day produced a story of heroism and gallantry that *every* American should know.

On April 10, 2003, the men of First platoon, Company G, Second Battalion, Fifth Marine regiment had been using Baghdad University as a place to sleep, organize, and maintain patrol. The battalion commander under whose leadership these men fell was ever watchful and ready to engage the enemy at all times. So when intelligence reports began to trickle in about possible Fedayeen fighters gathering near Baghdad in Tarmiya, Golf 2/5 was sent to check out the scene.

Martínez says the area was a mix of rural and urban: While there were wild, unkempt natural features, such as high grass along the roads, there were also several large, upscale homes. The marines had taken three amtracs (big metal boxes on tracks) with twenty-two guys smashed into each. Now just three miles away from the town of Tarmiya, locals could be seen frantically packing up and taking their possessions, seemingly their whole homes, with them.

One of the amtracs, Third Squad, was ahead of the others and had crossed the bridge that spanned a small river that led into town. Captain Hammond, who was in charge of Martínez and the rest of Golf Company, decided to have the two remaining amtracs wait to cross until he and the other officers had formed a tactical plan. They then began inching the amtracs closer to the more urbanized city that lay ahead.

"The place looked like a ghost town," Martínez recalls. "There was no one in there besides onesies and twosies [individuals on foot]. When you see a town empty like that, you know something bad is about to happen in Iraq. It means they [the Fedayeen] just kicked everyone out and that they're ready to rock 'n' roll with whoever is there."

Third squad's amtrac had now crossed the bridge and had begun entering the town. For the first ten minutes, everything seemed calm. Many of the marines began wondering whether they were on a bogus mission.

They weren't.

"Out of nowhere I heard about five or six RPGs go off and tons of AK-47 gunfire. Two of the RPGs got direct hits on third squad's track. The enemy was just waiting. Then they hit them."

The ambushed amtrac had been immobilized. Fortunately, most of the marines inside had already gotten out of the vehicle and begun reconnaissance along the roads. Two of the three-member crew—the gunner, the driver, and the mechanic—weren't so fortunate, however. One of the men had his calf muscle all but sheared off the bone. The bodies of the others were riddled with shrapnel.

The scene quickly morphed into something Martínez says could have come straight out of a movie, with enemy fighters popping out of windows in every direction. Then-Corporal Martínez, who at that moment was first fire team leader, was standing outside his amtrac. Martínez's squad leader and good friend, Corporal Timothy C. Tardif, was in charge.

The enemy force overwhelmingly outnumbered the marines. Worse, the enemy hadn't just hidden themselves inside the city that lay ahead; the insurgent enemy forces had also burrowed in the bushes and tall grass that lined the road and had begun charging the two Marine amtracs yet to cross the bridge with guns and RPG launchers.

"We just began picking off as many of the enemy as we could, especially those that had RPG launchers," remembers Martínez.

Finally, the first and second squad crossed the bridge into the town of Tarmiya. From inside the amtrac, Martínez could hear enemy bullets pinging off the amphibious assault vehicle (AAV) and RPGs screaming by just above the vehicle as it rolled into town. Dismounting the AAV, Tardif and Martínez pushed right, toward a series of buildings. With nothing to hide behind and Fedayeen popping up in windows and makeshift spider holes roughly fifty yards away, Martínez and Tardif were open targets. "Basically, it was the grace of God that we were getting by all this stuff. The rounds were coming so close that you could feel the heat and the snap of the round as it passed your ear. Today I have hearing loss because of that."

The torrent of enemy fire meant that Martínez and the others were depleting their ammunition. The men had worked their way through the swarm of enemy fire and toward a neighborhood cluster of seven homes about three hundred yards away from the rest of the platoon. Martínez, Tardif, and the others now had the unenviable task of clearing each house of the terrorists within.

The plan was to use the shouldler-launched multipurpose assault weapon (SMAW) gunners to blow a hole through the eight-foot adobe walls that surrounded each house. Once inside, however, the marines would be trapped. The only way to escape would be to kill the Fedayeen inside.

Tardif and a few others began setting up a shot to blast a hole through the first home's surrounding fence. Martínez stood ten feet away. "The next thing I know this guy [enemy fighter] sits up out of the bushes and lobs a grenade in our direction." The grenade literally bounced off Tardif's leg before detonating. But for the deafening ringing in his ears, Martínez went unscathed; Tardif wasn't so lucky.

"I could see Tardif's bone on his shin and thigh. He started bleeding profusely and turned white. I honestly thought he was going to bleed out and die. We didn't have a doc with us either. We decided not to do a tourniquet, because we didn't want him to lose his leg. So I had two of my guys patch him up really well. And at that point I instantly became in charge of the squad. We mowed down the guy who got Tardif. There was no way he was going to get away from us. And after that I had fifteen guys looking at me saying 'What next?' "

Having grown up listening to his father recount stories of great military leadership, this was a moment Martínez had been preparing for all his life. Like a quarterback in the huddle, Corporal Martínez looked his men in the eyes and commanded second fire team to stay outside the first house they intended to clear. "Don't let anyone enter that house once we [first fire team] are in. If you see anyone try to go in, shoot them."

The SMAW team took their shot at the wall, leaving a gaping hole in the adobe edifice surrounding the home's yard. Martínez and three others entered the house. The odds were stacked against them—fifteen terrorists versus four marines. Martínez and his men quickly switched from traditional to urbanized warfare combat. He says it was kill or be killed.

"The adrenaline was pumping pretty hard," said Martínez. "I had about sixty-five pounds of gear on and didn't even feel it. I didn't feel the heat. I wasn't getting tired. It felt like I was moving with nothing on. I was glad we were in this firefight because to me, the more enemy you eliminate the easier it gets farther down the road. But you have to understand, I had such a deep hatred for the cowards that did what they did [September eleventh] that you could say it was a joyous occasion for me because I was able to do my job and eliminate the enemy and do what we went there to do."

September 11 had made a deep impact on the then-nineteen-year-old marine, then serving in Japan. Like most Americans, Martínez says he was in shock. Yet *unlike* most Americans, he was eager to run *toward* the danger and not away from it. He had joined the Marines with the sole intention of seeing combat. In fact, he was so sure of his calling in life that had war not occurred, he says he would have kept reenlisting until he got his chance to see combat.

"War isn't glamorous by any means, but it was something I wanted to experience ever since I heard my dad tell me stories of his time serving in South America. To me, that's the definition of a man: a man going to combat and fighting for the United States. I was so mad that the terrorists could do that to people who weren't even a military target. They were just going to work in New York. And that solidified one hundred percent why I joined. I wanted to do something about it."

They had rid the first house of its fifteen terrorists, but other homes with an equal and greater number of terrorists remained. Looking over his shoulder, Martínez looked at his buddy, Tardif. His arms were now wrapped around the necks of the two marines lugging the injured leader around. Martínez feared Tardif was close to dying.

"He is such a strong guy," said Martínez. "Tardif said to me 'I'm not going to medevac until this is all over.' But he kept passing out from the blood loss every two minutes."

Tardif's heart and dedication were self-evident. But Martínez knew his friend, and he knew it was Tardif's wounds, not his

will, that were the problem. Martínez immediately established
communications with the other squads in the field. If he could
just get a break in the action, the squad could rush the fading
Tardif out of the battle zone to be airlifted.

The enemy, however, had other plans. The house across the
street began lighting up with gunfire. "We were on the roof of
the house, so we had to race down both stories of the house
while bullets ripped through the house."

Once in the yard, Martínez had two of the marines blast a
hole into the front of the second house, creating another gaping entryway. They would have to cross the street with enemy
snipers and fighters popping up all around them. Even if
Martínez's platoon laid down perfect suppressive fire, the
men would still be overwhelmingly outnumbered. One military analyst later estimated that the battle of Tarmiya had
been a company-sized enemy element against a platoon-sized
force. But, the newly minted leader wasn't thinking about battlefield statistics or even his own safety. He decided to race
across the street and into the smoldering hole.

The four men of first fire team went with him. Martínez
charged the opening in the wall and learned he had sorely un-
derestimated the number of enemy fighters in the enclosed
yard. He wondered whether he was about to die.

"If I would have died I wouldn't have been mad, because I
knew I would then be buried in Arlington National Cemetery
and be there with the guys who did that before me. That
wasn't a bad thought to me. . . . I told my mother before I left
that if I die not to be upset, because I'm not upset. I told her,
'I'll be buried with all my brothers in arms in Arlington.' She

started crying when I said it. But to me, that was a more comforting thought knowing that I would be dying for a good cause than, say, dying in a car accident."

Despite his inner peace about his fate, then-Corporal Martínez had no intentions of dying, and he was determined not to let Tardif or anyone else die either.

Running across the street and into the hole had been the equivalent of sprinting through highway traffic blindfolded. As soon as he and his closely huddled fire team stepped through the wall, insurgents began popping up like gophers from several spider holes dug into the enclosed yard. In the distance was a small guesthouse with five fighters inside alternating between loading and shooting.

Breaking through the hole, Martínez and his men began a rolling maneuver while killing as many of the enemy as possible. A few slender palm trees were the only features inside the yard to hide behind. Martínez, who at the time weighed 150 pounds, tried to make himself as skinny as possible behind one of the trees. A swarm of gunfire whizzed past both sides of his tree trunk. His eyes darted over at Lance Corporal Paul Gardner, who stood about seven meters to his left before glancing behind him at the wall he and his men had just burst through. The sight made his heart race. The only portion of the wall not riddled with bullets was a narrow twelve-inch patch that mirrored the outline of his palm tree trunk.

This was hardly the situation Martínez and his men had envisioned. The enemy was now just twenty-five meters away. The guesthouse-turned-bunker directly facing them was filled with fully armed Iraqi fighters. Worse, the marines' cache of ammo was dwindling. Something dramatic needed to happen and soon. Even though several of the enemy fighters hiding in the ground had been neutralized, the five shooters in the guest house were well protected and armed to the hilt.

Suddenly, Martínez, Lance Corporal García, Gardner, and Corporal Jaramillo heard a break in the action: The enemy gun from the guesthouse bunker had jammed. Martínez catapulted his body into action. As Gardner, García, and Jaramillo laid down suppressive fire, the young corporal leapt out from behind his palm tree and began a full-frontal charge toward the five shooters in the guesthouse. But as he was sprinting toward the bunker, Martínez heard the shooter's guns reengage and resume firing.

He was stranded.

He turned to break contact to a palm tree fifteen meters away. As he ran, the high school student who had gone jogging the night of his senior prom says he thought his life was about to end. His back was now a large moving bull's-eye.

"That was a moment when I thought for sure that I was going to get shot in the back and die," he said.

But he didn't. Instead, Martínez did something that to this day he says he can't fully explain. Racing toward the nearest tree, he had dragged his hand low to the ground and snatched up an enemy RPG launcher, one of the many weapons now strewn across the yard.

"I don't know why, but I picked it up. Whoever must have loaded the thing must have been an idiot, because they didn't lock the rocket in and it fell out. So I'm running along with the RPG in my hand and scooped up the rocket as well."

He scurried behind a different palm tree. With one good shot, he could destroy the building and free up his men, who, like him, were now pinned behind skinny palm trees.

"It was an RPG-7. I didn't know how to load a rocket. I mean, I'd seen one on TV and in pictures, but we weren't trained on how to use the enemy's RPGs. . . . So I had to learn on the spot."

The launcher proved awkward to handle and had an intricate dual-trigger system. When Martínez moved out from behind his tree and exposed himself to fire the rocket, nothing happened. "I decided to reload the rocket, check the sites, and put it on my shoulder. I exposed myself again. It still didn't fire. I thought to myself 'Is this thing a dud?'"

Martínez then noticed a feature on the trigger that he hadn't seen before. He decided to make a final third attempt.

"As soon as I moved out to expose myself and moved into position to fire the RPG, I heard Gardner, who was off to my left, get hit. He was hit in the ribs."

Corporal Martínez said Gardner's screams sounded like someone getting his arms sawed off. Seven meters from where Martínez stood, Gardner lay writhing on the ground in an expanding pool of blood. The Fedayeen zeroed in on the wounded marine, their gunfire punching holes in the ground surrounding his body.

"His face turned as white as Tardif's had. Blood was pouring out of his mouth. Later we realized that he had been paralyzed from the waist down, but at the time we didn't know. I thought to myself, *If I'm going to do it, I need to do it now. Because they're about to kill this guy if I don't.*"

Martínez steadied the grenade launcher, pointed it at the structure, braced for the kickback, and squeezed the trigger. The rocket whizzed across the yard and ripped through the building, producing a small blast. Of the five Fedayeen inside the bunker, the rocket had killed two of the shooters. More important, the kills bought Martínez and his men a ten- to fifteen-second break in the action, just enough time for the squad to drag the now-paralyzed Gardner out of the line of fire. But the remaining enemy fighters proved relentless. Even as the marines were moving Gardner to safety the Iraqi fighters had already resumed their assault and started shooting at Gardner and the marines dragging him to safety.

Corporal Martínez had had enough.

Martínez stood in front of Gardner like a shield. What he did next no one could have anticipated. With only fifteen meters separating him from the terrorists, Martínez mounted a full-frontal charge toward the guest house bunker.

Spraying his M-16 as he ran, after about fifteen rounds Martínez saw that the bolt on his weapon had locked to the rear. He was out of ammunition. The Fedayeen continued to shoot from the bunker's window openings and door, their bullets bouncing off the gear hanging from his body. With his M-16 out of ammo, he dropped the weapon, which hung from a sling around his body, and prepped a hand grenade for the last seven yards of his charge.

"While I was running toward the building and being shot at, I could hear them yelling in Arabic." Asked how he avoided being hit, Martínez replied, "Someone was with me. God said, 'He's not dying today.'"

As Corporal Martínez's body slammed against the outer

wall of the bunker, he threw the grenade as hard as he could into the open window that housed the terrorists who had paralyzed their marine brother, Gardner. The grenade's trajectory seemed to arc through the air in slow motion. With his back against the wall, Martínez looked up at the open window and waited for the blast.

"It was like a pink mist. I saw arms flying and legs flying. There was no outlet for that blast to go anywhere. It was like those guys got put in a blender . . . they were two feet away from me. The only thing that protected me was an eight-inch-thick adobe wall. Their blood was on me. My ears were ringing, and I had a really bad headache."

Silence fell over the yard. Martínez had single-handedly taken out the building and the fighters within. Many of the men in his platoon began securing the yard and checking weapons. Martínez reloaded his rifle and walked behind the structure he had just pulverized. Something moved. Out of the ground popped a Fedayeen fighter with his weapon drawn. In a scene reminiscent of the Wild West, Martínez drew his weapon faster and put down the enemy.

His men were astounded by all they had just witnessed. "Did you see what you did to those guys?!" they exclaimed. Martínez just shrugged and told them it wasn't even a question of what he intended to do. "I just couldn't let the guys who got my guy get away. Because then they're just going to go and do it again to someone else." As he later reaffirmed, "We're willing to die for each other and die for our country."

The rest of the company had heard the battle over the radio. Once there was a break in the gunfire, Captain Hammond had called in an amtrac and medevac chopper. While loading the nearly dead Tardif and Gardner into the vehicle, three enemy fighters had jumped out of some nearby bushes and began firing on the marines. The men took out the enemy in a brief two-minute firefight.

During his eight months in-country, Sergeant Marco Martínez had been in at least seven notable battles. But the one that took place on April 12, 2003, was by far the most intense. The fighting inside the houses had involved extreme close-quarter combat, often at arm's length. He'd been so close that he could see the enemies' eyes, hair, and even their teeth.

Yet despite the extreme danger Martínez and his platoon encountered, not one of the marines under Martínez's direction died that day, including both Tardif and Gardner. For his leadership and relentless strength and commitment to his marine brothers, Tardif was awarded the Silver Star. Gardner remains paralyzed from the waist down. Martínez says the marine's courage and tenacity that day were as strong as ever.

For his heroism and bravery, the U.S. Marine Corps awarded Sergeant Marco Martínez the Navy Cross, an honor second only to the Medal of Honor. A member of the Legion of Valor, he is one of only a handful of Hispanic Americans since Vietnam to receive the Navy Cross.

On August 21, 2003, Martínez left Iraq and headed back home to begin weighing his options. "It tore me apart for about three months, whether I should stay or get out. They offered me really attractive promotions. . . . But I had set some goals in my life, and one of them was to get my college degree. None of my family members that are male has a college education. They either work or go to the military and stay there. I wanted to be a marine. I wanted to go to war as a marine. And I did that. So I have decided that once I get my degree, perhaps I can go back as a commissioned officer."

Currently, Sergeant Martínez is a full-time psychology major at Saddleback College in Mission Viejo, California, with plans to transfer to either UCLA or Cal State Fullerton. Most of his college classmates and professors remain entirely unaware that they are in the company of an American hero.

"There are a lot of people in college who don't appreciate military service," says Martínez. "If someone asks me about it and I think that they're not too liberal, I might tell them I was in Iraq. But I don't tell them the full extent of it or anything about the Navy Cross. For example, a woman on campus had apparently learned I might be a marine. When I told her I was, she said, 'You're a disgusting human being, and I hope you rot in hell!'"

Marco Martínez remains steadfast in his determination to get his college diploma, but in his voice one can hear his love and pride for his marine brothers: "If North Korea happens, or things were to happen in Iran, I'm going to go back in. I miss it really bad," he told us.

The historic elections in Iraq and the full gravity of the Navy Cross have yet to fully sink in, says Martínez. Nevertheless, he feels honored to have been a part of shaping history: "When I have children, it feels good to know that they will be reading about one of the first free elections in a Middle Eastern country and that I had a chance to help in that."

Martínez knows firsthand the power of stories told in one's

youth passed from one generation to the next. As a young boy, Martínez had sat in rapt attention listening to his Army Ranger father tell stories about his time in battle. Today, his father listens proudly as his marine son shares stories of his own.

OFFICIAL NAVY CROSS CITATION

The President of the United States
takes pleasure in presenting
the Navy Cross
to

Marco Martínez
United States Marine Corps

for service as set forth in the following:

For extraordinary heroism while serving as First Fire Team Leader, 2nd Squad, 1st Platoon, Company G, 2nd Battalion, 5th Marines, 1st Marine Division, I Marine Expeditionary Force in support of Operation IRAQI FREEDOM on 12 April 2003. Responding to a call to reinforce his Platoon that was ambushed, Corporal Martínez effectively deployed his team under fire in supporting positions for a squad assault. After his squad leader was wounded, he took control and led the assault through a tree line where the ambush originated. As his squad advanced to secure successive enemy positions, it received sustained small arms fire from a nearby building. Enduring intense enemy fire and without regard for his own personal safety, Corporal Martínez launched a captured enemy rocket propelled grenade into the building temporarily silencing the enemy and allowing a wounded Marine to be evacuated and receive medical treatment. After receiving additional fire, he single-handedly assaulted the building and killed four enemy soldiers with a grenade and his rifle. By his outstanding display of decisive leadership, unlimited courage in the face of heavy enemy fire, and utmost devotion to duty, Corporal Martínez reflected great credit upon himself and upheld the highest traditions of the Marine Corps and the United States Naval Service.

4

Air Force Master Sergeant
William "Calvin" Markham
SILVER STAR

AFGHANISTAN

It was the grace of God. It was like we had a bubble over us.
—MASTER SERGEANT WILLIAM MARKHAM

When the final history of the War on Terror is written, Master Sergeant William Markham, a combat controller, will be remembered as the first member of the Air Force to set foot on Afghan soil. Just one month after the September 11 terrorist attacks, Markham, thirty-six, and his all-Army twelve-member team became among the first U.S. Special Operators to enter Afghanistan. Their mission: assist the Northern Alliance in destroying the Taliban, secure the capital city of Kabul, and liberate the country.

"The Taliban would unleash everything at us," remembers Markham. "We took enormous amounts of fire: small-arms fire, tank rounds, you name it. They also had ZSU-23s, an antiaircraft weapon, and turned them on us sending, what looked like large, flaming footballs at our position." When

asked how he and his twelve-man special ops team—
Operational Detachment Alpha Team 555, also known as
"Triple Nickel"—survived the torrent of enemy fire, the airman's answer turns heavenward: "It was the grace of God,"
says Master Sergeant Markham. "It was like we had a bubble
over us."

A member of the little known Air Force Special Tactics
group, Markham is one of only four hundred special operations forces (SOFs) who serve on this elite team. Their training is similar to that of the Navy SEALS, Army Rangers, or
Green Berets. Less than one percent of all recruits who enter
special tactics training will finish.[1] "The special ops family is
a world apart. We are a much smaller family of soldiers," says
Markham. "It's like being picked to be on the varsity team."

But growing up in Waukesha, Wisconsin, Markham's all-
star status was far from guaranteed. In fact, one might say it
was even unlikely. "I had decided I didn't want to work at the
foundry, the local industry. And I knew I didn't want to spend
the rest of my life as the second-best pool player in Waukesha" (a friend of his being the first). So with no military history in his family's background, he decided to set a family
precedent, and he wasted no time doing so.

Waukesha North High School, the school where Markham
graduated, held its commencement ceremony on June 8, 1986.
As fate would have it, his birthday is June 9. So the day after
graduation, an eighteen-year-old William Markham, who also
goes by the nickname "Calvin," traded his cap and gown for
an air force uniform, the military branch that he believes takes
the best care of its members.

During his first five years in the service, Markham's focus

had been on security police work. Until one day the 6 feet 1, 250-pound airman was approached about trying out for special operations. At the time, Markham says the physical tests included a 1,500-meter swim, completing 65 push-ups in under 2 minutes, a timed 3-mile run, and 70 sit-ups in 2 minutes. A thrill seeker by nature, he accepted the challenge and went on to join the ranks of the elite Air Force SOFs.

Combat controllers are responsible for infiltrating enemy lines, mapping and plotting targets, pinpointing exact coordinates, and selecting the best bombs and aircraft to destroy the enemy. They then communicate directly with pilots overhead to ensure pinpoint accuracy, often while being pummeled by enemy fire. Following his combat-control training, Markham was sent on missions that took him to places like Africa, Bosnia, and South America. So when Markham received word he would be attached to an army special operations team, he felt confident he was ready for the mission.

"You've been training for this your whole life. Sure, the first thing that runs through your mind is 'Does someone not like me and is sending me on a suicide mission?'" he joked. "But when the call comes it's what we call 'game-on.' You've got a job to do. The game is on."

On October 19, 2001, for Markham and his team, it was, indeed, game on.

Just nineteen days earlier Master Sergeant Markham had flown from Hurlburt Field, Florida, to Karshi-Khanabad, Uzbekistan, where he served as team leader for the Combat Search and Rescue teams (CSAR). It wasn't until October 15, just four days before his mission, that he learned he would be part of the twelve-man team that would be the first to enter Afghanistan. True to the USAF Combat Control motto, then-Tech Sergeant Markham would be "first there."

"When you're the only Air Force guy, your teammates have some fun with you. But I have worked with army special forces in the past and knew several of the SF guys from SOF dive school training. So when I walked into the tent to meet up with my team, Team Sergeant Greg McCormack looked up at me and said, 'Hey, swim buddy.' So we all came together as a unit quickly."

Once in-country, the team assembled at Bagram Airfield. For two weeks, A-Team 555 "Triple Nickel" was the only SOF team working on the ground behind enemy lines. During their twenty-five days of intense action, Markham and his team underwent experiences that would change them, as well as history, forever.

Triple Nickel's first task was to link up with Northern Alliance fighters, a group who opposed the Taliban and whose knowledge of the local area could prove vital. Markham remembers the initial meeting of his team and the rebel fighters.

"The Northern Alliance? Those guys are great! At first, they were a bit standoffish. It wasn't that they didn't trust us; it was just that they didn't really understand how we could help them. Some of them didn't even know 9/11 had happened, so we tried to explain it to them. But soldiers are soldiers; we have a common bond."

That bond would soon be strengthened when Markham's team, working with the Northern Alliance leadership, settled on a Taliban command and control building as their first target. Unbeknownst to the terrorists below, Triple Nickel and their Northern Alliance counterparts had been spying on them high above from a mountain ridge.

"I called in the first CAS [close air support] of the operation and a Navy F-18 arrived over the area. I talked the pilot in to the first target. He dropped ordnance and hit the building.

"I turned to my teammates and said, 'We just made history. We just made the first strike against the al Qaeda.' It was a great feeling," says Markham.[2]

The combat controller explained that any awkwardness or uncertainty on the part of the Northern Alliance was erased after that first air strike. "The wall was broken, and they seemed to realize we were there to help them."[3] To foster even greater trust and respect between Triple Nickel and the Northern Alliance, Markham says he and his teammates remained committed to live like their hosts. That included growing beards, longer hair, and eating the local cuisine.

"We went in with only three days' worth of food supplies. Our re-supply went bad. Over a million dollars worth of food and support materials were destroyed when the parachute blew up in mid-flight," said Markham. Despite efforts to salvage the supply drop, the items proved unrecoverable. So Markham and his teammates were forced to eat a steady diet not commonly found in his hometown of Waukesha, Wisconsin: goat and rice.

"Yeah, I won't be sad if I never have to eat goat and rice again," Markham confessed. But the airman says it was all apart of achieving what SOFs are all about: "Winning hearts and minds."

Another way of winning the trust and support of the

Northern Alliance soldiers involved putting American muscle where its mouth was in the form of consistent and lethal air strikes. Over the next twenty-five days, Markham says he ordered up virtually every U.S. aircraft on his CAS menu, including F-18s, F-15s, F-16s, B-1s, and B-52s. "We probably called in anywhere from five to twenty CAS calls a day. The valley was literally filled with tanks, personnel carriers, and military sites."[4]

Being first on the ground also encouraged a curious mix of old and new warfare technologies. For example, while making his way toward Kabul, Markham's high-tech equipment stood in sharp contrast to his mode of transportation. Air Force Chief of Staff General John Jumper explains:

What we found in Afghanistan is that the young sergeant— Sergeant Markham—on the ground riding a *horse* with the warlords of Afghanistan as a special operator, stopped and set up his tripod with his keyboard and his laser goggles and took a sighting on the enemy positions on the next ridge line and beamed them up to the B-52s, which then put a string of bombs down that ridge line and took out two hundred al Qaeda in one pass and had the warlord tell the young sergeant, "I've been doing this for fifteen years, and I've never seen that many of my enemy die at one time in my life."[5]

During the last day of operations, one Northern Alliance fighter expressed his gratitude for Master Sergeant Markham in the most profound way one can: by protecting Markham's life with his own. While positioned atop a two-story building, Markham's team came under intense enemy fire, including small-arms fire and tank rounds. As the team moved down off the roof, one Northern Alliance soldier laid his body on top of the combat controller. Markham says that he later asked through an interpreter why the man had leapt on top of him and pinned him to the ground. The Northern Alliance fighter explained that were he to die, the fight could go on. But were *Markham* to die, the group's ability to call in planes and destroy the enemy would die with him.

The next day, coalition forces and the Northern Alliance entered the Afghan capital and secured the city. Markham and his SOF team then took a trip to the only place that reminded them of home, the American embassy. Since 1989, the structure had been evacuated and deserted. "We gained access," remembers Markham, "and one of the first things I saw was an American flag. It was on top of a pile of straw. Someone had tried to destroy it; the straw was burnt but the flag had somehow gone untouched—not a burn mark one."[6] The twelve-man team unfurled the flag and stood on the steps of the wartorn U.S. embassy for a picture. Upon returning home, Markham presented the flag to his unit.

In the end, Master Sergeant Markham's July 2, 2003, Silver Star citation credited him with directing 175 sorties, which resulted in the elimination of 450 enemy vehicles and the killing of more than 3,500 Taliban fighters. But in the wake of Afghanistan's historic elections, "Calvin" Markham, the kid from Waukesha, considers himself lucky to have been given the chance to serve his country and the now liberated people of Afghanistan.

"We volunteer to do this," he told us. "It is one of my greatest rewards in life. It's changed me. I've become a better person. It makes me want to be a better leader for my team, a better father. I've achieved my personal goal in life. I've got peace of mind."

Asked how he feels when he hears critics of the War on Terror and those who oppose the sacrifices being made by America's armed forces, Markham says he feels no spite; quite the contrary: "I do what I do to keep this country free. So when I hear that kind of thing, honestly, it makes me glad, because it means those individuals have the freedom to think and say what they wish. . . . The media are sometimes a little like how some people are when watching a NASCAR race: They're waiting for the crash. They're waiting for the bad thing to happen. But basically I think they're armchair quarterbacks. They don't see the bigger picture of what we're trying to do.

"The Taliban was ignorant. We're trying to give the children a chance. We are giving the people—the children—the freedom to decide the fate of their future."

OFFICIAL SILVER STAR CITATION

The President of the United States of America
authorized by Act of Congress July 9, 1918, has awarded
the Silver Star

to

William Markham
United States Air Force

for service as set forth in the following:

Technical Sergeant William C. Markham distinguished himself by gallantry in connection with military operations against an armed enemy of the United States near Kabul, Afghanistan, from 14 October 2001 to 30 November 2001. On 21 October 2001, within forty-eight hours of the detachment's arrival in Afghanistan, Sergeant Markham planned, organized, and led a close air support reconnaissance mission to within two kilometers of the Taliban front line in order to identify potential observation posts from which his team could execute missions. Almost immediately upon arrival, Sergeant Markham's team came under direct enemy fire from tanks, mortars, and artillery. Despite heavy incoming fire, in which numerous rounds impacted within fifty to seventy-five meters of his position, Sergeant Markham instinctively and successfully directed multiple close air support sorties against key Taliban leadership positions, command and control elements, fortified positions, and numerous anti-aircraft artillery sites. Throughout this highly successful mission, Sergeant Markham skillfully directed multiple air strikes involving over one hundred seventy-five sorties of both strategic and attack aircraft resulting in the elimination of approximately four hundred and fifty enemy vehicles and over three thousand five hundred enemy troops. The resulting close air support operations were decisive in supporting the Northern Alliance ground offensive, which resulted in the successful liberation of the capital city of Kabul and led to the eventual surrender of hundreds of al Qaeda and Taliban ground forces. Sergeant Markham's valor and calmness under enemy fire were a constant source of inspiration to his detachment and General Fahim Khan's Northern Alliance forces. By his gallantry and devotion to duty, Sergeant Markham has reflected great credit upon himself and the United States Air Force.

5

Army Master Sergeant Patrick Quinn
SILVER STAR

IRAQ

As I wear it the rest of my life, I'll always think of the guys I
was with, not what I personally did.

—MASTER SERGEANT PATRICK QUINN

Of all the men whom one would select as the most likely to
become a soldier, perhaps none was more suited than Patrick
M. Quinn, thirty-three, who, as a boy, knew his destiny and
followed it with the same passion and purpose as the soldiers
his family had produced before him. Some men find their calling late in life; Quinn knew his from the start.

In the tranquil town of Cromwell, Connecticut, Marilyn
Pitruzzello, Patrick Quinn's mother, remembers how her son
liked to spend his afternoons once school let out. "All [he] did
was play army all day long," Pitruzzello recalls. "He would
buy the army helmets and swords. That's what he always
wanted to do."[1]

Young Quinn's passion for all things military was so apparent that even his next-door neighbor, City Council Member

Stan Terry, remembers the junior "boot camp" the boy built in his backyard: "He was friends with my son; I watched him grow up," says Terry. "He built a foxhole in my backyard. You could have parked a Jeep in this thing."[2]

After graduating from Cromwell High School, Quinn put down his backyard shovel, storebought swords, and helmet and headed off for the army to experience the real thing first-hand. It was a decision he had made all his own, yet the example had been set by others. Continuing his family's heritage of service, Quinn would soon join his grandfather (a soldier who served in World War II) and his uncle (who fought in Vietnam) as a war veteran when he was called into battle during the first Gulf War.[3] There, he honed myriad skills while serving in various units. Being exposed to so many tasks revealed in Quinn abilities he never knew he possessed. Others noticed as well. His steady judgment, humble and quiet demeanor, relentless work ethic, and ability to execute multiple skills simultaneously made him the quintessential candidate for the Special Forces.

Just as the men in Quinn's family represented a lineage of service, so too did his assignment to Company A, Second Battalion of the Tenth Special Forces Group (SFG) reflect a historic precedent: The Tenth SFG is America's oldest Special Forces unit. Since their inception, Special Forces have always been important, but no one could have predicted the vital role they would play on the post–September 11 battlefield. Indeed, much has been made about SFGs by military analysts, and rightly so. Unlike any other divisional-sized unit, the U.S. Army Special Forces Command (USASFC) is not located in one centralized location. Instead, these forces are spread out from coast-to-coast and throughout the world.

The army's requirements for Special Forces consideration are both mentally and physically rigorous. Patrick Quinn's temperament, adaptability, and discipline, however, were custom-made for mastering the five doctrinal missions of special forces operations: foreign internal defense, unconventional warfare, special reconnaissance, direct action, and counterterrorism. These diverse objectives mean Special Forces are frequently engaged in all three stages of the operational continuum: peacetime, conflict, and war. In addition to mastering the art of clandestine and covert methods of unconventional engagement, Special Forces are trained in linguistic, political, and regional matters to assist with humanitarian relief and improve human rights conditions. The breadth of knowledge and varied skill set required of Special Forces officers makes these soldiers uniquely prepared to meet the complex challenges posed by terrorism. These "Renaissance men" of the American military have a singular credo, one that captures the overarching purpose of America's entrance into Operation Iraqi Freedom: *De Oppresso Liber*—To Free the Oppressed.

The depth of Master Sergeant Patrick Quinn's commitment to this code would be tested when, as the leader of his twelve-man team, he was charged with coordinating with a group of Kurdish militia to battle an Iraqi armored unit April 2–5, 2003. Directing a group of soldiers with whom you are familiar is hard enough; coordinating with a foreign militia would require bridging cultural and linguistic chasms. Yet Sergeant Quinn's greatest challenge existed not within his *own* ranks; it was the size of the opposing forces that was the real reason for concern.

Quinn's detachment faced off with the Iraqi Fourth and Sixteenth Infantry divisions, the Iraqi Ninety-sixth Infantry Brigade, and a battalion of Fedayeen Saddam (literally "Men of Sacrifice") fighters. Considered among the fiercest and most loyal of Saddam's supporters, Fedayeen were directed by Uday Hussein, the now-deceased son of the former Iraqi dictator. The brutal, thuglike tactics employed by the Fedayeen fighters made them an especially unpredictable enemy. This group, for example, organized itself into "death squads" and was responsible for shooting fleeing Iraqis in the back to send a message to those who would seek refuge away from battle-torn areas. Even with the technological advantages Sergeant Quinn and his men possessed, they were severely outnumbered. The Army's official Silver Star citation notes the overwhelming odds and fierce resistance Quinn's men encountered as they fought their way toward the city of Mosul.

When the smoke cleared, the soft-spoken Sergeant Quinn was credited with leading his detachment in the destruction of two enemy tanks, four armored personnel carriers, thirty Iraqi soldiers, the neutralization of the Iraqi Fourth and Sixteenth Infantry divisions, the destruction of the Iraqi Ninety-sixth Infantry Brigade, the routing of a Fedayeen Saddam battalion, and the seizure of thirty kilometers of ground.

For Sergeant Quinn's leadership, he, along with four other soldiers from various outfits, were awarded Silver Stars during a ceremony in Washington, D.C., just one day before the second anniversary of the September 11 terrorist attacks on the United States. Quinn, who now makes his home in Colorado with his wife, Holly, spoke on the phone to his mother prior to attending his Silver Star pinning.

"All I got from him is, 'I'm getting a medal,'" said Marilynn Pitruzzello.[4] When she asked him to elaborate, true to his modest nature, Quinn wouldn't. All he would say was that the medal was for simply doing his job. Although Pitruzzello feels the accolades her son received were well deserved, she says medals do not motivate him. Instead, she says it is his love of service—a passion he developed as a young boy dreaming of one day entering the military—that compels him to be a better soldier.

One person who doesn't mind singing Quinn's praises is Helen Sullivan, his sister. "I think my brother's just an amazing human being. I am so proud of my brother, I can't even put it into words," she said. Although exceedingly proud of Sergeant Quinn's battlefield heroics, the family is glad he's home. Tom Pitruzzello, Quinn's stepfather, confesses he feared for his stepson's safety. "I was scared, but I had a lot of confidence in his training. And he knows what he's doing," he said. Pitruzzello also added that Sergeant Quinn's success never surprised him. "Just what his niche in life would be I wasn't sure," said his stepfather. "But I always had the feeling that Patrick was going to do something. He was never afraid of anything. He was a go-getter."[5]

Standing in the nation's capitol, Army Chief of Staff General Peter Schoomaker pinned the Silver Star, the award given for "gallantry in action against an enemy of the United States," over Patrick Quinn's heart. After touring the D.C. area, Quinn would receive another special invitation when Secretary of Defense Donald Rumsfeld requested that he and the other Silver Star recipients assist him in laying a wreath at the Tomb of the Unknown Soldier at Arlington National Cemetery. Remembering the efforts of the men who came before him as well as the victims of September 11 was deeply important to Quinn.

Patrick Quinn believes in the importance of never forgetting the sacrifices of others. When asked about the significance of his actions and what his Silver Star represents to him, he said, "To me, it's a tribute to everything that my [detachment] did during our fighting in Iraq. As I wear it the rest of my life, I'll always think of the guys I was with, not what I personally did."[6]

Master Sergeant Quinn says he worries that Americans aren't getting the full story about the successes in Iraq. He believes the media have failed to provide citizens with a balanced picture of the events in the War on Terror. "There are a ton of amazing soldiers in the army, and they're doing amazing things every day," he said. "And a lot of that story's not getting out."[7]

Quinn feels that the perceptions of the soldiers on the ground in contrast to those of Americans watching Operation Iraqi Freedom unfold on television are probably very different. Through the eyes of soldiers on the ground, the reopening of schools and hospitals are common, everyday occurrences. However, Americans back in the States, Quinn believes, would be surprised to learn of the regularity with which these events are taking place in Iraq.

As for life back in the town of Cromwell, Connecticut, things there have changed, too. Town officials declared October 14 Patrick Quinn Day. Fittingly, it was First Selectman and former neighbor Stan Terry, the man whose backyard provided a young boy with a makeshift boot camp, who read the proclamation in Quinn's honor during a ceremony held at town hall. Also fitting was the fact that Master Sergeant Quinn was unable to attend the ceremony, an event that would have undoubtedly made him uncomfortable. Military duty was in his blood, and he believed he was just doing his job. What Patrick Quinn failed to realize, however, was that most jobs do not require the risking of one's life nor the certain knowledge of armed conflict. Still, when it comes to his heroics in Iraq and the Silver Star he received, Quinn's mother, a woman who always knew her son would grow up to be a soldier, captured Sergeant Quinn's wishes best when she said flatly, "He doesn't like anybody to make a fuss over it."[8]

OFFICIAL SILVER STAR CITATION

The President of the United States of America
authorized by Act of Congress July 9, 1918, has awarded
the Silver Star

to

Patrick Quinn
United States Army

for service as set forth in the following:

For gallantry above and beyond the call of duty, MSG. Quinn showed unrelenting courage while ODA 065 engaged and destroyed the Iraqi 96th Infantry Brigade, neutralized the Iraqi 4th and 16th Infantry Divisions, and routed a battalion of Saddam Fedayeen. MSG. Quinn's performance was integral in the 2nd Battalion, 10th Special Forces Group (Airborne) attack towards Mosul, Iraq. His actions under overwhelming odds and fierce resistance are a great credit to him, the 10th Special Forces Group (Airborne) and the United States Army.

6

Marine First Sergeant Justin LeHew
NAVY CROSS

IRAQ

We're just marines. This is what we do. A six-year-old kid trying to beat cancer—*that*'s the fight of your life; *that*'s a hero.
—FIRST SERGEANT JUSTIN LEHEW

There is a sound to sagacity, a cadence to wisdom. Listen to
Marine First Sergeant Justin LeHew speak, and you will hear
it. His words reveal a mix of ferocity and forgiveness. He has
seen the best and worst of humanity. In his hands he has held
both the severed leg of a dead marine and the hand of a dying
Iraqi woman. Yet one thing is clear: this man is marine to his
core. Aside from being at home with his wife, Cynthia, and
their daughter, Aisley, there isn't any place First Sergeant
LeHew would rather be than watching over his "boys."

His paternal instinct is, in many ways, a reflection of the
voice that spurs him on: that of his father. It's out on the battlefield that memories of his dad often flash through his mind.
"I think of him all of the time," says First Sergeant LeHew.

"You're in the middle of it all, and you hope he's looking down and saying 'Good job, boy. I'm honored to call you my son.'"

LeHew's father died when he was thirteen years old and rests in Arlington National Cemetery. The memory of the funeral ceremony has stayed with LeHew to this day. Indeed, his father's passing was the beginning of a lifelong journey to honor and rediscover the man taken from him at such a young age.

On June 6, 1944, LeHew's father had been part of the first wave of the Normandy invasion when, as an infantryman in the Twenty-ninth Division, he found himself on Omaha Beach. LeHew says he still remembers the vague and often humorous answers his father would give when he would ask him about his time in battle. But after he passed away, Lehew would learn the truth: His father had lived through one of the most hellish and heroic moments in U.S. military history. Indeed, his dad had been one of only three men to survive when their boat was wiped out just minutes after their ramp was lowered.

As General Omar Bradley once said, "Every man who set foot on Omaha Beach that day was a hero." Yet it wasn't until LeHew's siblings saw the motion picture *Saving Private Ryan* that they fully understood the horrors their father had experienced firsthand. For Justin LeHew, his father's sacrifice and dedication to duty had set a soaring standard to live up to, a tradition to keep alive.

"I tell my boys [marines] all the time, two things brought every one of us here. We either had something to prove to ourselves or somebody else. That's what people come into the Marine Corps for. For me, it was a little bit of both. I wanted to prove it to myself, because I was a little runt. And two, I wanted to live up to the military history of my family."

On March 23, 2003, then Gunnery Sergeant LeHew got his chance to do just that. His unimaginable bravery and heroism in the face of overwhelming odds were overshadowed by several events that unfolded that day, including the story of Jessica Lynch and her ambushed unit, whom LeHew and his men rescued. What's more, the friendly-fire incidents that occurred two miles north of his position at the Saddam Canal Bridge (covered in the chapter on Navy Hospitalman Third Class Luis Fonseca, Jr.) diverted media attention from the heroes who had risked everything for their brothers. That hardly bothered LeHew, however. Like his father, he doesn't talk much about his heroic actions. Still, Navy Crosses aren't awarded haphazardly; a heart-rending story of uncommon valor lies behind each one. As Lieutenant General James T. Conway told the Marine Expeditionary Unit (MEU) men who attended First Sergeant LeHew's award ceremony, "This is something you'll probably never see again. This is second only to the Congressional Medal of Honor."[1]

In effect since April 1917 and established by an Act of Congress on February 4, 1919, the Navy Cross may be awarded to any person who, while serving with the navy or marine corps, distinguishes himself/herself in action by extraordinary heroism not justifying an award of the Medal of Honor.

According to the U.S. Marine Corps, the action must take place under one of three circumstances: while engaged in action against an enemy of the United States, while engaged in military operations involving conflict with an opposing foreign force, or while serving with friendly foreign forces engaged in an armed conflict in which the United States is not a belligerent party. To earn a Navy Cross an individual must have performed in the presence of great danger or at great personal risk. What's more, the action must have been executed in such a manner as to render the individual highly conspicuous among others of equal grade, rate, experience, or position of responsibility.

As his story reveals, in life and deed, First Sergeant Justin D. LeHew embodies and exceeds these criteria.

It was March 23, 2003, and the temperature in Nasiriyah that day was a squelching 120 plus degrees, and that's without the 60 pounds of gear marines lug across the battlefield. At the time, LeHew was an Amphibious Assault Platoon sergeant for Company A, Second Assault Amphibian Battalion, attached to the First Battalion, Second Marine Regiment, Task Force Tarawa. Moving into Nasiriyah that morning, his column of twelve amphibious assault vehicles (AAVs or "amtracs") were led by an M1-A1 Abrams tank unit. A deceptively reassuring report had just come over the radio net the night prior: Eight thousand Iraqis in and around the city had thrown down their arms and surrendered.

The roughly 160 marines of Alpha Company had dismounted miles outside of the city in the early morning hours and had begun clearing the small farms that led into Nasiriyah. That's when LeHew received a strange report: U.S. Army soldiers were supposedly in the field in front of them.

The report seemed odd. LeHew, who was riding in the last AAV in the column, had been told their task force was spearheading the drive and that there was no one in front of them.

Even more curious was the fact that the reports indicated the army soldiers were not in vehicles but were on *foot*. LeHew was directed to take two vehicles forward and check out the scene for himself. Along the way, he asked some marines whether they had seen any army soldiers. "What are you drinking?!" they said. "We haven't seen any army soldiers for days."

After advancing 2.5 kilometers, however, the picture became clearer. "All of the sudden, we pass these American vehicles that are on fire in the center of the road. They were still flaming. It was a tanker, a wrecker truck, various support vehicles, and a couple of Humvees."

First Sergeant James Thompson, who had been riding in LeHew's AAV by chance, happened to glance back to his right at the field. Approximately two hundred meters away, five army soldiers were waving their hands wildly. Then, about one hundred meters away, they spotted another group of five. Scattered Iraqi fighters were still in the area firing AK-47s and small-arms fire. LeHew and his men sped to the first group of soldiers. One of them, a warrant officer, said half of his group, roughly thirteen soldiers, were unaccounted for. LeHew later learned that one of these individuals was Army Private Jessica Lynch, but in the thick of the action, his focus was on tending to the wounded soldiers. One had four gunshot wounds spaced from each leg to his ribcage to his arm; another had a gunshot wound to the back of his leg; and another was hit but stable.

"We put our corpsmen with their medics. I thought their medics were doing an excellent job. A lot of the army later said that the reason their soldiers had lived was because of my marines. Even though it was hard for a marine to say this,

I told them that if it wasn't for those army medics, those guys would have bled out. They did everything in the middle of those firefights to stabilize these people and survive."

Iraqi fighters had hidden themselves down in the rolling grassy terrain and were now popping off shots at the soldiers and their marine rescuers. That's when LeHew jumped up into the weapons station of his AAV, gripped his .50-caliber machine gun, and began laying down suppressive fire to cover the loading of the wounded soldiers into the second AAV, forcing the enemy shooters to retreat back into the industrial-style buildings on the outskirts of the city. Although he had no way of knowing how many Iraqis might be inside the distant city, the buildings looked like they might prove difficult.

The marines loaded up the soldiers and drove them back down the road. Word had it that there was an ambulance in the area. After finding the big red cross, LeHew and his men dropped the ramps, unloaded the soldiers, and briefed the medical team on the status of their wounds before rejoining their marine platoon. It was about seven A.M.

Following the rescue effort, LeHew and his men received word they would be moving up. The city of Nasiriyah was still too far to be seen with the naked eye, but as they crept closer, palm trees, huts, and city-style construction became more discernible. A U.S. Marine artillery battery was already in position. Before entering a potentially hostile zone, these groups often launch artillery at enemy installations from a distance. When combined with air strikes, these efforts can significantly "soften up" enemy strongholds.

"Gunny, why aren't they [the artillery teams] shooting into the city?" one of the gunnery sergeant's men asked.

It was a good question, and LeHew didn't quite know how to answer; he was wondering the same thing. The artillery teams were already *fire capped.* That's the term an artillery commander uses to tell the battalion commander that he's loaded and ready to fire. Stranger still, the teams had been fire capped for over thirty minutes and had requested permission to fire numerous times but were told to stand by. The decision had already been made to put infantry into the city and secure the bridgeheads. This would happen before the battery even got to fire one round. It was a critical decision.

Writing on the "catalogue of errors" that occurred at Nasiriyah, renowned military historian John Keegan wrote:

Careful planning failed, in circumstances fortunately unique during the Iraq War, to deliver the desired result. There was to be an unforeseen battle for Nasiriyah and it was to take a messy and costly form, seized on gleefully by anti-American elements in the Western media to demonstrate that the war was not going the coalition's way. The marines had anticipated trouble in Nasiriyah. They had even coined the term "Ambush Alley" to describe what they expected there. Trouble came but not of the sort anticipated. . . . Nasiriyah was chosen by the Ba'ath party and Saddam's various militias as a productive place in which to stage resistance.[2]

Although the U.S. military didn't know it at the time, three brigades of Iraqi troops—roughly twenty thousand enemy fighters—had burrowed themselves in buildings and under the streets of Nasiriyah. The massive, hidden "hive" of enemy fighters buzzed with anticipation, and First Battalion, Second Marines, which numbered roughly one thousand marines, would soon be ordered to ram its boot straight into the middle of it. Worse still, they would do so without tank units leading the way.

"We heard over the radio that we were going to put infantry into the city. To me, that was the furthest thing from my mind. I thought, and all the rest of us thought, we're going to hit this city with artillery, and we're going to hit it with air [strikes], because you always prep the target before you send in ground troops."

LeHew, however, is the forgiving sort who strives to see things through the eyes of others. He stresses that at the time, no one knew of the hell lurking inside the city, and no signs of extreme hostile intent had yet been shown. Although he would have done things differently, he says he recognizes the dilemma of those at the top. Therefore the decision not to light up Nasiriyah with air strikes and artillery had been made with caution—some might say *too much* caution—for possible nonhostile Iraqis on the ground.

Finally, the order came over the radio: LeHew's group, Alpha Company, was to capture and hold the all-important southern bridge, which led into the city. Without it, other forces, such as Charlie Company, would be unable to press northward to capture and hold the Saddam Canal Bridge.

There was just one snag: The four M1-A1 Abrams tanks leading LeHew's column were almost out of gas and had been sent to be refueled. The AAVs, however, were told to press on anyway. Whatever the reason, one thing was clear: The thin-skinned AAVs would enter the building-lined streets of Nasiriyah with little more than two inches of metal plating between themselves and the outsides of their vehicles.

LeHew says everyone was in a high state of alert, adrenaline racing. "We were just outside the city, and this van drives up. I hear over the radio net my marines scream 'Sagger!' All the vehicles in the column began to zigzag back and forth just as I had instructed them to do in training. I see a van with an enemy fighter inside fire the rocket. I can see the guy himself. He was driving away from us, and I could see him hanging out of the back of the van and the trail coming from the rocket. He couldn't have been more than fifty to seventy-five meters away."

The rocket skipped across the road and missed LeHew's column. "That's when all the boys realized, *We're in this. This is dangerous. They have rockets, and our vehicles can't withstand those rockets.*"

The marines couldn't get to the enemy van, but they didn't want to break contact. So they sped on toward their objective: the southern bridge. But for a pop here and there, the area surrounding the bridge was silent. An eerie calm fell over the place. One- and two-story buildings hugged the sides of the city streets.

LeHew's column of twelve AAVs rolled forward and crossed the southern bridge without incident. Their job was to hold and secure the bridge and buildings to assure safe passage for the marines traveling through their position. The vehicles fanned out in three sections, with four amtracs in each, and were spaced approximately fifty meters apart. The marines emptied out of their AAVs and were now performing clearing movements while huddled against the walls of the buildings surrounding them. LeHew's vehicle, still in the rear of the column, planted itself at a four-way intersection.

"No one was shooting. It was quiet. And it seemed really weird," remembers LeHew. "That lasted about seven minutes. And then all at once, at the eighth minute, it was like the entire world exploded. Everything came crashing down on our heads all at once."

A hurricane of RPK machine-gun fire, small-arms fire, and RPGs swept through the streets. LeHew rotated his gun turret and yelled commands to his platoon and infantry. The streets were so flooded with enemy fire that four rockets flew through the intersection at one time. The marines on the ground scrambled for cover. That's when LeHew heard something tumble end over end above his head. His eyes darted up and locked on the object in mid-flight. It was an RPG. The grenade smacked the ground twenty meters behind his vehicle and exploded. Somehow, not a single marine was injured.

LeHew whipped his head around and saw a blur of flashing lights. An Iraqi ambulance was now careening toward his intersection. The gunnery sergeant and another vehicle's gunner fired warning shots. But the ambulance kept barreling straight toward his AAV. So both marines let their .50-caliber machine guns rip and lit up the vehicle's cabin, killing the driver and front-seat passenger. When the ambulance swerved off the road, out of the back jumped six fighters clad in black, all with weapons in hand.

"From that point on it was full-throttle for four and a half hours. They were in the houses, in the alleys, on top of buildings . . . they were everywhere. Cars started racing over the bridge. We fired warning shots, but they wouldn't stop, so we started shooting the cars on the bridge. People would then run out of the cars and under the bridge, which we later learned had been stockpiled with weapons, and begin shooting at us. When you looked down the alleyways, you could see them huddling in big groups with weapons. They started to look like Somalis in Mogadishu moving in waves. They now knew we're embedded down there and they're starting to encircle us. There had to have been hundreds of them."

Knocking out enemy fighters with an impressive display of lethal accuracy, LeHew and his boys blasted away at every place they saw fire. In a situation like this, one might assume that civilians would be cowering inside their homes. Not so. Many of them had come out of their houses to watch the firefight unfold.

"I could not believe that. Women, kids . . . I can distinctly remember seeing two guys sitting on a veranda drinking tea and watching the entire firefight happen."

In an odd way, it was a compliment to the Americans' commitment to fight fairly and take painstaking efforts to avoid Iraqi civilian casualties. Some of the civilians, however, were not so kind in returning the favor. By their own choice, or perhaps because of the threat of force against them, LeHew said the enemy fighters were using women holding babies as spotters to locate and kill marines.

Meanwhile, up the road, the first and second sections were experiencing problems of their own. The second section, headed by Sergeant Justin Smith, was experiencing weapons malfunctions from the MK-19 40mm grenade launcher and M-2 .50-caliber machine guns. The long ride through the dusty desert had jammed the guns and rendered many of them useless. The AAV crewmen compensated by grabbing their M-16s and 9mm pistols and lying on top of their vehicles to hold off enemy fighters.

On down the road, the first section, led by First Lieutenant Brenize and Sergeant Keith, had been pummeled with RPG gunners while trying to set up the counter mortar team. The marines laid down suppressive fire to protect the mortar men.

"We were starting to see that this is turning into a really bad situation," said LeHew. "I'm in my vehicle hitting the people coming over the bridge. All the infantry is on the deck. The company commander, Captain Mike Brooks, is on the deck and running from position to position dragging his radio operator, Lance Corporal Miles, with him. He was a *phenomenal* commander."

While Captain Brooks was doing everything he could to get much needed tank and air support, LeHew and his men were still receiving massive amounts of fire and rockets from the windows of the buildings staring down over them. All of a sudden, LeHew's driver, Private First Class Edward Sasser, noticed something bizarre.

"Look at those dumb asses!" said Sasser, now pointing at the AAV driving past them. "They're heading in the wrong direction [toward the southern bridge], and they didn't even put their ramp up!"

The AAV's metal ramp was scraping the street, sending sparks jumping up off the ground. *That better not be one of mine*, LeHew thought to himself. *Who in the world would drive without permission in the wrong direction with the ramp down and the men inside exposed?*

"The next thing I saw was two rocket trails and a marine on fire fall out of the back of the vehicle. The vehicle came to a halt right in front of our position," said LeHew.

The AAV belonged to Charlie Company, the group just to the north, who had been charged with capturing and securing the Sadaam Canal Bridge. The marines there were ensnared in a horrendous firefight that ultimately claimed the lives of eighteen marines. The now-flaming AAV had nine injured marines inside and was trying to rush them back across the southern bridge to receive medical treatment.

With the flaming vehicle now in the center of LeHew's intersection, he sat in disbelief for a brief second. Burning marines began falling out of the AAV. To no one in particular he said, "No one is running toward that vehicle."

"It was just instinct at the time. I jumped up out of the turret. My sergeant mechanic, Scott Dahn, was in the back. I said, 'Dan, get in the turret.' Here he was, a maintenance chief, now finding himself in a weapons station. I also had a hospital corpsman in the vehicle with me, Alex Velásquez. I said, 'Doc, come with me.' We got outside. I remember to this day how stupid I was. I didn't even have my helmet on! We were running around out there with no helmet, no weapon, and no ammo."

LeHew and Velásquez sprinted through the fire zone and raced toward the smoldering AAV. A blinding plume of black smoke poured out of the vehicle. With mortars, RPG, and machine guns blasting all around him, LeHew ran to the vehicle's ramp.

"The first thing I see on the ramp is the leg of a marine. It was completely severed off. I picked it up and handed it to

Doc. I told him, 'Lay this off to the side. Hopefully we'll find the guy that owns this.' It still had the boot on it and had been blown from the knee down."

Both men crawled inside the AAV and were met with the closest thing to hell either of them had ever seen. The amtrac was strewn with the body parts of marines.

"I remember seeing one marine on the right side of the vehicle. Doc had gone to take his pulse, and I remember saying, 'Forget it, half his head is missing.' I picked up an ear that was lying on the bench seat and told Doc to hang onto it. From what I could tell everybody in the back was dead, at least that's what I thought at the time."

When the Iraqi RPGs had ripped through the vehicle, the troop compartment had caved in on itself and crushed and severed the limbs of many of the men inside. The AAV's fuel tank had also been hit and had soaked the dead marines and their grenades and ammo with gasoline. LeHew and the corpsman raced to triage as many bodies as they could. LeHew struggled to untangle the knot of gear and body parts. Outside he could hear the firefight raging. He knew he and his corpsman were sitting on a powder keg. One more enemy RPG was all it would take to ignite the AAV–turned bomb. LeHew snatched as many weapons as he could find and began wading through the carnage on his way to destroy the vehicle's radios to prevent them from falling into enemy hands.

"As I was crawling through all that stuff into the center, I stepped on something and actually heard someone gasp for air. I didn't know where it was coming from. So I started digging around and underneath, bent in a V position, was a live marine."

It was the unconscious body of Corporal Matthew Juska from Charlie Company. First Sergeant LeHew had never met the young man. He doubted whether he would live. But he was a marine, and that meant LeHew was determined to do everything in his power to increase his injured brother's chance of survival.

"No matter who he is—whether he's black or white, whether he hates you or is racist—it doesn't matter: No marine will ever let another marine lie on the battlefield wounded. He will risk his own life to pull that other marine to safety. It doesn't matter who they are," said LeHew.

The entire length of Corporal Juska's head had been split open. LeHew turned to platoon corpsman Velásquez. "Give me a knife, Doc." LeHew then lashed away at the tangle of gear. Velásquez poked his head out the back of the AAV. "We need some help here!" he yelled. Faintly, LeHew and Velásquez heard someone yell back, "You're f—king crazy! You're all going to die in there."

The comment enraged LeHew and his corpsman. Doc Velásquez, however, wasn't going anywhere. "I'm here as long as you're here, Gunny," he told him.

The two men worried that by moving Corporal Juska's body they might kill him, but they had no choice. The AAV was a sitting duck, and they'd been inside the vehicle for almost an hour now. Velásquez squeezed the skin on Corporal Juska's head together to keep it from splitting apart while LeHew tugged on the stuck and dying marine. Juska seemed large, unusually large. LeHew later found out that at six feet six, Juska was the largest marine in the entire company. First Sergeant Thompson then showed up with a couple other marines to help. The men formed a human chain, each of them pulling on LeHew, who in turn had latched on to Corporal Juska's body. Finally, he had pried the marine loose.

Stepping out of the mangled AAV, they ran the wounded marine seventy meters through the fire-swept intersection to the back of LeHew's AAV. LeHew could hear marines screaming for medevac helicopters. The refueled Abrams tanks had just arrived and were blasting away at enemy positions. The company executive officer (XO), Lieutenant Matt Martin, and Sergeant Jason Cantu had a house off to the side of the street about eighty meters from LeHew's position that was now being used as a medevac site.

LeHew looked down the alleyways. Waves of enemy fighters were coming toward him. Up on top of the roofs he could see Iraqis with RPG launchers. "Gunny, we've *got* to get him out of here! He's gonna die if we don't," Velásquez urged.

LeHew wanted to check out the medevac house first before putting Corporal Juska through a risky run through the fire zone. Weaponless, he sprinted over to the house. Several casualties were inside. Some of the marines were so dazed they couldn't respond. Others had blood pouring out of their ears and noses. Marines were running in and out of the house, but to LeHew's surprise, no one was tasked with defending the wounded marines. Worse, the house had only been *partially* cleared; enemy fighters were still hidden inside the building. Just as he wouldn't abandon Corporal Juska, LeHew refused to allow his wounded brothers to fall into enemy hands.

"You could hear Iraqis in the back of the house talking," LeHew remembers. "My first instinct was, 'We need to defend this house!'"

Dodging enemy fire, LeHew ran out into the street and gathered weapons. A young marine, gray from head-to-toe, hobbled up to him inside the house. The young man had a couple of nasty leg wounds. His communications helmet let LeHew know he was an amtrac crewman.

"He looked up at me and said, 'I can still fight, Gunny. I want to stay here.'"

Allowing a wounded marine to defend other wounded marines was the last thing he wanted to do, but Lehew had no choice; he needed to get back to Corporal Juska, and there was no one else to defend the house. So LeHew gave the gritty young marine a rifle and positioned him inside the doorway of the house.

"Look," LeHew told him, "I've got to go back out there to take care of some business. If anyone comes from my direction, don't shoot. If anyone comes from the opposite direction, shoot them."

LeHew ran back through the fire-filled street to his AAV and Corporal Juska. The zone reminded him of Armageddon. He thought of the scene his father must have seen while wading onto Omaha Beach on D-day. God had spared his father. He prayed He would do the same for him.

LeHew screamed over the radio net to his platoon commander, First Lieutenant Brenize, that they needed an air medevac. The battalion XO, Major Tuggle, said a helicopter was on its way. LeHew and the major began clearing a landing zone on the road away from the intersection and marked it with purple smoke, the only color they could find. The CH-46 touched down and LeHew and his marines began moving Corporal Juska toward the CH-46 helicopter. As they were

moving toward the bird, the CH-46 picked up without warning and flew directly over their heads and landed again one
hundred meters away and directly adjacent to the intersection.
Unbeknownst to the pilot, this was the least desirable and
most dangerous spot on the battlefield, as the intersection was
still hot with small arms, RPK, and RPG fire. LeHew and his
marines had no choice but to turn Corporal Juska around and
run him back the distance through the fire-swept intersection
to the helicopter.

The confusion had been the result of an infantryman who
had set off some green smoke just after LeHew's purple
smoke. Green smoke, it turned out, indicated it was safe to
land.

"I hope that pilot got a Distinguished Flying Cross because
that was one of the hottest zones. It had power lines, buildings, debris, and poles all around it," LeHew recalled.

The pilot flying the CH-46 was Major Eric García who, at
the time, was attached to Marine Medium Helicopter Squadron-
162, Marine Aircraft Group-29, Third MAW. On March 1, 2005,
Garcia was indeed awarded the Distinguished Flying Cross.
According to his medal citation, Garcia had flown 16.7 hours
over a 24-hour period, led the evacuation of 23 casualties and
5 enemy prisoners while flying bravely into four contested
landing zones. One of those zones belonged to LeHew. "This
happened during the first few days of the war," said García,
"so I had no idea what to expect. The thing I am most proud of
is that we were all just doing our jobs and by that, we were
able to get those marines home safe."[3]

With rockets and small-arms fire ripping through the air,
First Sergeant LeHew, Corpsman Velásquez, First Sergeant

Thompson, Major Tuggle, and a few more marines ran Corporal Juska to the helicopter. At the same time First Lieutenant Martin and a second group started removing the injured marines from the house and escorted them to the awaiting medevac bird.

"Corporal Juska was the last person we put in the helicopter. No sooner had my foot stepped off the back end of that helo, did the crew chief say 'Drop him. We'll deal with him.' They yanked Corporal Juska inside, and the last thing I saw when the bird was about a hundred feet in the air was Corporal Juska's legs dangling out of the back of the bird," said LeHew.

The southern bridge was now secure, but their work was far from finished. They loaded into their AAVs and headed north. LeHew was as exhausted and dehydrated as he'd ever been. His situational awareness, however, was as sharp as ever.

While making their way through Ambush Alley, LeHew didn't like the looks of things. "The enemy had all the advantage points. They were firing so many weapons from the rooftops and streets, it's a miracle nobody died in that convoy," said LeHew.[4]

What this humble marine failed to mention was that he had ordered his vehicles to drive 35 mph and to fire their .50-caliber machine guns at the tops of the buildings to keep enemy shooters' heads down. Because of First Sergeant LeHew's quick thinking and decisive leadership, his unit was not hit while traversing the dangerous zone. But more miraculous than that was the fact that in all of Alpha Company, not a single marine had been killed. As for Corporal Matthew Juska from Charlie Company, First Sergeant Justin LeHew's determination to save a fallen brother had paid off. Today, Corporal Juska is alive and well.

Tragically, the same could not be said for eighteen men from Charlie Company engaged in the brutal firefight north of the Saddam Canal Bridge (discussed in the chapter on Navy HM3 Luis Fonseca, Jr.). LeHew's men helped secure the area that Charlie Company fought to hold. He saw friends, fellow gunnery sergeants, who'd been hit or killed. That night LeHew didn't sleep or eat.

In the weeks following the horrendous firefights in and around Nasiriyah, LeHew led and witnessed other efforts—all of which were much less visible—that would further reveal this warrior's heartbeat and love for his "boys." This compassion, however, wasn't just reserved for American forces; it extended to the Iraqis who had been hurt on the battlefield as well.

"The biggest challenge mentally and morally for my marines came when we had to treat Iraqi personnel that were shot. . . . Seeing the compassion of these boys was amazing." In the week to follow, First Sergeant LeHew and his men treated or evacuated seventy-seven Iraqi casualties, including some enemy combatants who, only moments prior, had been shooting at LeHew and trying to kill his marines. Others, however, had simply been in the wrong place at the wrong time.

"One lady especially sticks out in my mind," LeHew said. "She was a mom and had been shot six times. She was going to die. We all knew this. That night, I went over there and just held her hand until she passed away. There was an interpreter there. She had no resentment. She understood."

Thankfully, many of the innocent civilians suffered wounds

that were much less severe. But at night, when his marines sat around talking, LeHew could hear some of his boys talking about Iraqis who had been injured and wondering how they were doing. So whenever it was time for a food or mail run, First Sergeant LeHew would send a marine who had helped rescue an injured Iraqi to give each marine an opportunity to check up on that person's recovery status for himself.

These weren't the kinds of stories the mainstream media and critics of the War on Terror liked to publicize. Yet, again, LeHew's forgiving nature shines through: "I don't blame them. Everyone is ignorant to a certain extent. People are real easy to cast stones at things they don't understand. . . . You can't blame people for their ignorance; you just hope you can educate them."

LeHew says the only thing he asks from the critics is that they support the men and women who give them their right to dissent. "You don't ever bad-mouth the players on your home team. You can say that you feel that this war is unjustified or whatever, but you support the home team, the American servicemen in the fight."

Support for the home team. That, First Sergeant LeHew believes, is at the core of America's strength and compassion for the oppressed. Like the father he barely knew who left footprints in the sands of Omaha Beach, Justin LeHew strives to leave footprints of peace and security in the sands of history. It's what motivates him most.

"It's all the crosses in Arlington Cemetery. It's all those GIs who died over there with my dad on Omaha Beach. You want your generation to do America justice just like that one did, and I believe we are doing just that."

The President of the United States
takes pleasure in presenting
the Navy Cross
to

Justin LeHew
United States Marine Corps

for service as set forth in the following:

For extraordinary heroism as Amphibious Assault Platoon Sergeant, Company A, 1st Battalion, 2d Marines, Task Force Tarawa, 1st Marine Expeditionary Force in support of Operation IRAQI FREEDOM on 23 and 24 March 2003. As Regimental Combat Team 2 attacked north towards An Nasiriyah, Iraq, lead elements of the Battalion came under heavy enemy fire. When beleaguered United States Army 507th Maintenance Company convoy was spotted in the distance, Gunnery Sergeant Lehew and his crew were dispatched to rescue the soldiers. Under constant enemy fire, he led the rescue team to the soldiers. With total disregard for his own welfare, he assisted the evacuation effort of four soldiers, two of whom were critically wounded. While still receiving enemy fire, he climbed back into his vehicle and immediately began suppressing enemy infantry. During the subsequent company attack on the eastern bridge over the Euphrates River, Gunnery Sergeant Lehew continuously exposed himself to withering enemy fire during the three-hour urban firefight. His courageous battlefield presence inspired his marines to fight a determined foe and allowed him to position his platoon's heavy machine guns to repel numerous waves of attackers. In the midst of the battle, an Amphibious Assault Vehicle was destroyed, killing or wounding all its occupants. Gunnery Sergeant Lehew immediately moved to recover the nine marines. He again exposed himself to a barrage of fire as he worked for nearly an hour recovering casualties from the wreckage. By his outstanding display of decisive leadership, unlimited courage in the face of heavy enemy fire, and utmost devotion to duty, Gunnery Sergeant Lehew reflected great credit upon himself and upheld the highest traditions of the Marine Corps and the United States Naval Service.

7

Navy Hospital Corpsman Third Class
Luis Fonseca, Jr.
NAVY CROSS

IRAQ

If you're worried about dying out there, instead of treating
your marines, you're in the wrong business.

—HOSPITALMAN THIRD CLASS LUIS FONSECA, JR.

To most people, the battlefield is a place for killing, a death
zone. But Luis Fonseca, Jr., isn't most people. "I never wanted
to harm people. I always wanted to help people," said Fonseca.

While fully prepared to defend his brothers and himself at
a moment's notice, Navy Hospitalman Third Class Fonseca
views war zones from a vantage point that's different from
most. To him, the battlefield can be a place of healing, a place
to utilize his specialized medical training to support his marine brothers as they wage war on terrorism.

At only 5 feet 5, 140 pounds, HM3 Fonseca does not con-
form to the stereotypical image of the jut-jawed military war
hero. He was unquestionably among the smallest men in battle March 23, 2003, in Nasiriyah, Iraq, when he saved the

lives of numerous marines. As former director of Central Intelligence, Jim Woolsey, told a packed audience during a speech, while Fonseca might have been one of the smallest in size, he "was not the smallest in heroism. It is because of him, and enlisted men like him, that we can be here tonight."[1]

Growing up in Fayetteville, North Carolina, Luis Fonseca's father had been an army first sergeant. Fonseca says his dad never went into much detail about what he did. Today, when HM3 Fonseca's own two sons ask him what he does, he follows the model set by his father: "Daddy's out there to help his friends in case they get hurt," he tells them. "He's helping to look for the bad guys so they don't come over here and hurt us anymore."

During high school, Fonseca gravitated toward classes in math and science. He was particularly fascinated by topics related to the field of medicine. Still, his interest in these subjects was not strong enough to prevent him from dropping out of school his senior year. "I didn't want to be one of the guys that just stayed at home and didn't do anything with his life. I wanted to do something with myself and achieve some sort of accomplishment," explained Fonseca. "I later received my GED while I was in the navy."

Ironically, it was while taking a test that Luis Fonseca realized the navy was the place for him. While taking his Armed Services Vocational Aptitude Battery (ASVAB), a sailor at the testing site caught his eye.

"There was a navy guy in there wearing his working blues; not his dress blues but his working blues. We all thought he was an officer or something, and I asked him what branch he was in. He said the navy. I was in there with all my buddies and told them, 'Someday I'll be wearing that uniform.' So, actually, it was the uniform that drew me to the navy." He chuckled.

Fonseca's longstanding interest in all things medical drew him to the job of hospital corpsman. His training taught him how to perform a litany of lifesaving skills, spanning a wide spectrum of medical knowledge, including: administering immunizations, inserting IVs, preparing medical records, performing tracheotomies, and treating dehydration, myriad wounds, frostbite, trench foot, fractures, and all forms of shock. In this respect, hospital corpsmen are similar to civilian medics. Where they differ, of course, is the circumstances under which they are expected to save lives, circumstances where their *own* lives are in as much danger as those they seek to save. It's hard to imagine entering a war zone without having one's weapon drawn, but even though hospital corpsmen are permitted to carry rifles or other arms, Fonseca says he demands that his hands be free.

"If you're laying down fire, you're not doing your job . . . you have to attend to your casualties. You have to put all your trust in your fellow marine that he's going to keep you safe while you're working on your brother who's lying on the ground hurt and injured."

On March 23, 2003, that's precisely what HM3 Fonseca did. Armed with nothing more than a standard-issue 9mm pistol, Fonseca risked his own life to save his marine brothers. The battle to capture the Saddam Canal Bridge would claim the lives of eighteen Americans. But had it not been for Luis Fonseca's heroism and valor, that number would have surely been much higher.

HM3 Luis Fonseca had been in country three days now and had yet to see any action. "My friends began joking, 'I guess this is what combat's really like. We could do this all the time,'" Fonseca remembers.

His fourth day started out slow. Charlie Company, First Battalion, Second Marine Regiment rolled along in a column of amphibious assault vehicles (AAVs or "amtracs") led by several M1-A1 Abrams tanks. While traveling on the road leading to the outskirts of Nasiriyah, Fonseca stood up and surveyed the war-torn terrain. As he scanned the earth before him, he saw Iraqi tanks and mechanized elements blazing on the roadside. They had been hit by American attack helicopters, which had rained lethal firepower down on their positions. Fonseca's vehicle stopped just short of the southern bridge that crossed over the Euphrates River.

Waiting for the order to cross, the tanks from their column got diverted to assist another area. Fonseca heard Platoon Sergeant Tom Meyers verify the command: They were to push north to capture the Saddam Canal Bridge, but they would have no tank support. This was a problem. While their mounted .50-caliber machine guns were powerful, they were nothing compared to the M1-A1 Abrams tanks, which typically spearhead a column. Having no tanks leading the charge meant they would be vulnerable.

As they crossed over the southern bridge and headed north through the urbanized area often called Ambush Alley, the Iraqis alongside the road gave them the thumbs up. But distinguishing friendly civilians from enemy fighters could prove difficult. Not only were they often dressed similarly, but enemy fighters had mastered the art of subterfuge by blending into areas filled with noncombatants. Still, if the Americans could make it through the building-lined streets, they would be only a few football fields away from reaching the object of their mission: the Saddam Canal Bridge. It was just a little after eleven thirty A.M. Fonseca stood up inside his medevac AAV.

"Get down!" someone yelled.

Fonseca ducked. Bullets plinked off the metal walls of his AAV. But he still wasn't convinced they were in danger. The sounds of small-arms fire had become "background music," and within minutes, the line of vehicles had made it through Ambush Alley and across the Saddam Canal Bridge. Charlie Company was now on an elevated road with ditches on either side. Low-lying grassy fields, which provided perfect cover for enemy forces, stretched beyond the ditches. Fonseca's medevac amtrac swerved to the right into a ditch and then jerked back up onto the road. The other amtracs in the column fanned out over roughly a quarter-mile-wide area.[2]

In minutes, mortars, small-arms fire, and RPG blasted away at the tankless column. Surrounded by grassy fields on both sides, and with the city not far behind them, Charlie Company was ensnared in an attack on all sides.

"About five minutes later, I heard 2/11 had been hit with an RPG . . . over the intercom someone said, 'Doc, 2/11 has been hit. I need you to go out there and see what's going on,' " said Fonseca.

The five-foot-five, one-hundred-forty-pound hospital corpsmen snatched his thirty-five-pound camouflaged medical bag and 9mm pistol, the only weapon he carried.

"Right before you step out of the AAV, you think about your family for a split second. But as soon as that door opened and I jumped out, I ran straight toward 2/11. I saw Sergeant Matthew Beavers and asked him if his guys were okay. He said that five marines were hurt and to tend to those casualties."

Since the medical evacuation amtrac typically brings up the rear of a column, Fonseca's vehicle was over three hundred meters—three football fields—away from the injured marines. Mortar fire, small-arms fire, and RPG zipped across the open road Fonseca would be forced to run. Like a running back huddled behind his lead blockers, Fonseca protected his bag with his life and ran behind the marines in front of him who laid down suppressive fire. The rucksacks hanging outside his AAV had been hit by enemy fire and now looked like flaming, charred marshmallows stuck to the outside of his amtrac. But Fonseca's focus remained on protecting the life-saving contents of his medical bag. In it, he carried everything from basic medicines, like Tylenol, all the way to morphine. Splints, battle dresses, IV fluids, hemostats, sutures, and scalpels had also been stuffed inside.

When he got to the injured marines they were lying beside their burning amtrac. The Fedayeen Saddam, Baath Party loyalists, and Iraqi fighters had scored a direct RPG hit. The blast had lifted the amtrac off the ground and ripped open the aluminum walls surrounding the marines inside. The fire threatened a possible secondary explosion from rounds cooking inside the vehicle. Fonseca looked down at the tangle of bloody flesh. This wasn't like the drills back at Camp Lejeune, North Carolina, he thought to himself. This was the real deal.

The marines who had run in front of him and provided

Fonseca with cover quickly dashed off to find and kill enemy fighters. Fonseca got to work. Calmly and methodically, he treated his first two casualties, Corporal Randy Glass, a twenty-year-old from Pennsylvania, and Corporal Michael Mead, twenty, from Michigan. Although still conscious, the detonated grenade had partially amputated their legs. The men were in enormous pain and screaming. "Don't worry," Fonseca told them, "We're going to get you bandaged up and get you the hell out of here."

The hospital corpsman staunched the bleeding, which he describes as having been profuse, with tourniquets and bandages. Like most corpsmen, Fonseca has a stomach made of steel, a necessary trait for the job. But the pulpy mass of shredded flesh looked bad, really bad. "Honestly, if I would have pulled out my knife, all I would have had to do was cut a few muscles, some skin, and some more veins, and their legs would have been fully amputated," said Fonseca. As Corporal Glass later told CBS News, his leg looked "like Freddie Krueger's face."

Fonseca's plan was to establish a casualty collection point inside his medevac vehicle. With all five casualties now stabilized, he gathered others in the area to help carry the five injured marines for the three-hundred-meter trek back to his amtrac. He slung his medical bag over his shoulder before hoisting Private Jason Keough, Buffalo, New York, over his back in a fireman's hold and ran like hell.

The sight was something to see. The 5 feet 5, 140-pound Fonseca had a 6-feet, 210-pound marine draped over his back and was now dodging enemy fire all the way. "I guess it was adrenaline," says Fonseca. "We are taught the proper way to transport a patient. But in a situation like that, you get them there however you can get them there."

With the five marines now inside the medical evacuation vehicle, Fonseca directed the other hospital corpsmen to reassess each patient's condition. They treated eyes for flash wounds, reapplied bandages, and inserted IVs. Corporal Glass and Corporal Mead were in agony. Fonseca says it is not uncommon for a patient's pain to overwhelm him once he is removed from the immediate danger zone. Once the initial shock wears off, patients process the experience and gain greater sensitivity to their body's condition. When this happens they can experience a tidal wave of pain. So much so that after reexamining Corporal Glass and Corporal Mead, HM3 Fonseca approved them for morphine. Fonseca pulled out a black marker and scrawled "1231" on each marine's forehead to indicate the time he administered the pain medication.

"When you feel like you're safe, that's when it really starts to hit you, and guys really start to break down. Thoughts go through your head that you're not going to make it. The patients will comfort each other, though. Private Keough did a great job comforting his buddies and saying 'Hey, don't worry. Doc's gonna take care of us and get us the hell out of here alive. Once we get out of here, the drinks are on us. Don't worry about it.' That's one of the big things you have to do once you stabilize a patient: You have to comfort them. You have to let them know that everything is going to be all right and that you're going to get them out of there."

With the bonds of support strong and the patients stabilized, things inside the vehicle had begun to seem relatively calm and under control. Outside, however, the firefight raged on; marines were being killed. That's when Fonseca got the call that another amtrac, 206, needed help. He would leave the nurturing confines of his makeshift hospital and reenter the fire zone.

This time there were no marines to provide him with cover. Fonseca broke protocol and dashed through the fire zone alone. It was crazy, and he knew he could get chewed out for it, but he didn't care. He was determined to treat every last patient. "I was going to do my job until I got hit," said Fonseca.

Some of the vehicles had already reverted back across the Saddam Canal Bridge. That meant the vehicle sequence had been shuffled and was out of order. Fonseca raced up and down the road frantically searching for injured marines.

He approached one group and asked whether they were okay and if they knew the whereabouts of 206. "Hey Doc. We're doing good," they replied. Yet none of them seemed to know anything about any injured members of 206. Fonseca wasn't taking any chances. He sprinted south through the zone and ran straight up to the company commander. The commander told him the report might have been a miscommunication and to return to his medevac vehicle. Fonseca and another corpsman turned to run. The company commander stopped them. "You're doing a great job. Keep it up," he said.

When he returned to his medical evacuation vehicle, Fonseca confirmed that the report had indeed been a mistake; 206 was fine. What wasn't fine, however, were the Iraqi mortar blasts creeping closer and closer to Fonseca's makeshift hospital. It was every hospital corpsman's worst nightmare: to retrieve casualties from the battlefield, stabilize them, make them comfortable in a vehicle and ready to be rushed out of danger with the next break in the firefight, only to have the hospital on tracks immobilized or worse.

The nightmare became a reality: The first mortar landed fifteen meters from Fonseca's amtrac, sending shockwaves rippling through the vehicle.

The Iraqis had found their range. A second mortar blast slammed into the side of the vehicle and rocked the patients inside, but the enemy wasn't through. A third mortar landed directly on top of the vehicle and exploded. The corpsmen looked at each other and leapt into action.

"I tried to establish communications with the driver to get us the hell out of there, but our communications had been disabled. So I immediately decided to get my five injured marines out of the vehicle so they wouldn't be injured in the next blast."

As soon as the amtrac door opened, a fourth blast, this one from a recoilless rifle—a devastating antiaircraft gun—slammed inside the vehicle. When Fonseca woke up he was dazed, his ears muffled. Somehow he managed to regain composure and kept working.

"I grabbed Corporal Mead and Corporal Glass and pulled them out of the amtrac and dragged them over to a ditch. We got the other guys out of there and sent them on their way with other corpsmen."

Fonseca refused to leave Corporal Glass and Corporal Mead alone. Their veins now raced with morphine, and there was no way of knowing how long it would be until they could be transported out of the zone. He had been the one to first tend to their partially amputated legs, appendages that dangled from little more than the stringy strips of sinew and flesh still attached. He had told the men they were going to be okay, that he would see to it that they got out, and he wasn't about to give up on them now. Marines are trained to protect their field docs. But the lightweight medic would now swap roles; he would watch over his marines. There, in a ditch in Nasiriyah, with mortars, small-arms fire, and RPG exploding all around them, the three men waited for an amtrac and the chance to evacuate.

"I replay that part a lot in my mind. Sometimes when I think about it, it seems like it lasted fifteen to thirty minutes. Sometimes it seems like hours. But it was a while, since the firefight lasted around six hours. I told them that I wanted to go find them an amtrac. But they said, 'No, Doc. We're sitting ducks. We don't want to be back in one [amtrac].' I said, 'All right. We can stay right here in the ditch then and see what happens.'

"We talked about everything: about not getting overrun by the enemy, how if an enemy comes, we won't get taken as POWs; we'd rather go down fighting. But I was the only one who had a weapon, and all I had was my 9 mm. . . . I thank God I never had to pull out my nine."

The three men were as different as the states from which they had come: Pennsylvania, Michigan, and North Carolina. But in that moment, Fonseca felt they were all the same. Their lives were in each other's hands.

Suddenly, their ditch began to rumble. It was an amtrac that had been cleared to move. Fonseca sprang to his feet and tracked the vehicle down. He lifted one of the men into the amtrac, another marine helped lift the other. HM3 Fonseca hopped into the AAV with Corporal Glass and Corporal

Mead. The driver drove south until they came across Second Battalion, Eighth Marines. They found an ambulance, and Fonseca jumped out and flagged down another corpsman. He relayed the information regarding his patients' wounds and condition before saying good-bye to the men whose lives he'd helped save. As the ambulance sped away, Fonseca loaded into another vehicle to rejoin his company and the fight.

The firefight ended as the sun dropped heavy in the Iraqi sky. Eighteen marines had been killed during the battle to hold the Saddam Canal Bridge. Tragically, some of the deaths had been the result of friendly fire from an A-10 Thunderbolt (aka Warthog) that had strafed the zone in an attempt to pick off enemy fighters.[3]

That night, Luis Fonseca slept in another amtrac, his having been destroyed after the fourth devastating blast. It was cold that night. All his gear had been destroyed except for his beloved medical bag. Some of the others loaned him a sleeping bag and some gear. But as he tried to sleep, he replayed the events of the day in his mind. He wondered how he had been spared. He had exposed himself so brazenly—some might say carelessly—with nothing more than a pistol. And yet others who had been better armed and who had stayed in their positions had died. The thought bothered him. Deeply.

"I think about it. I'm more of a believer in the good will of God than in luck. I thought about the situations I had put myself in and how much I had exposed myself. Corpsmen aren't supposed to expose themselves as much as many of us did that day. I just know that the good Lord has a plan for everything. . . . He has the master plan in His hands. If he wants me to come home, I'm going to come home."

As for Corporal Glass and Corporal Mead, at the time of this writing, HM3 Fonseca has not had an opportunity to speak with either of them. But like any good doctor, he has managed to track his patients' medical rehabilitation and progress through intermediaries, despite having been redeployed to Afghanistan and Iraq. Miraculously, both marines' legs were saved, and each continues to make a steady recovery.

A CBS News reporter interviewed Corporal Randy Glass and asked him whether he blames President George W. Bush for his injuries. "I blame the commander in chief of every Iraqi," Glass shot back. "Not the commander in chief of the Americans."[4]

Likewise, while fully aware of the enormous challenges that still lie ahead, HM3 Fonseca says he supports the way the president responded in the wake of 9/11: "I'm glad our commander in chief took the time to figure out what was going on and plan accordingly. . . . I do think we are making a difference, but unfortunately this is going to be a long process."

During an August 11, 2004, Camp Lejeune, North Carolina, awards ceremony, Secretary of the Navy Gordon R. England had this to say about HM3 Fonseca: "I feel privileged to be here to recognize Hospitalman Fonseca for his extraordinary valor and courage. Corpsmen have a long tradition of service to the United States Marine Corps. You make all of us proud, and let me personally thank you for going above and beyond the call of duty. On behalf of the president of the United States and all of America, I thank you."[5]

HM3 Fonseca was humbled and surprised when he learned

he would receive the Navy Cross, the second-highest award a sailor can receive next to the Medal of Honor: "I don't feel like I did anything special," Fonseca said. "I did what corpsmen have been doing for two hundred years . . . I wasn't the only one in that firefight . . . I think all the guys in that firefight should be highly decorated and honored as well."

María Fonseca, Luis's wife, is filled with pride for her hero husband. She understands the life of hospital corpsmen more than most. After all, she's a navy corpsman herself. Sometimes, back home in Camp Lejeune, North Carolina, María teases her husband that she's considering reverting back to her maiden name so she won't have the burden of living up to the heroic standards of the Fonseca name. When she says it, Luis just laughs.

"All I did was my job. I just wish I could have done more."

*The President of the United States
takes pleasure in presenting
the Navy Cross
to*

**Luis E. Fonseca, Jr.
United States Navy**

for service as set forth in the following:

For conspicuous gallantry and intrepidity in action against the enemy while serving as Corpsman, Amphibious Assault Vehicle Platoon, Company C, First Battalion, Second Marines, Regimental Combat Team 2 on 23 March 2003. During Company C's assault and seizure of the Saddam Canal Bridge, an amphibious assault vehicle was struck by a rocket-propelled grenade inflicting five casualties. Without concern for his own safety, Hospitalman Apprentice Fonseca braved small arms, machine gun, and intense rocket propelled grenade fire to evacuate the wounded marines from the burning amphibious assault vehicle and tend to their wounds. He established a casualty collection point inside the unit's medical evacuation amphibious assault vehicle, calmly and methodically stabilizing two casualties with lower limb amputations by applying tourniquets and administering morphine. He continued to treat and care for the wounded awaiting evacuation until his vehicle was rendered immobile by enemy direct and indirect fire. Under a wall of enemy machine gun fire, he directed the movement of four casualties from the damaged vehicle by organizing litter teams from available marines. He personally carried one critically wounded marine over open ground to another vehicle. Following a deadly artillery barrage, Hospitalman Apprentice Fonseca again exposed himself to enemy fire to treat marines wounded along the perimeter. Returning to the casualty evacuation amphibious assault vehicle, he accompanied his casualties South through the city to a Battalion Aid Station. After briefing medical personnel on the status of his patients, Hospitalman Apprentice Fonseca returned North through the city to Company C's lines and to his fellow marines that had been wounded in his absence. His timely and effective care undoubtedly saved the lives of numerous casualties. Hospitalman Apprentice Fonseca's actions reflected great credit upon himself and upheld the highest traditions of the Marine Corps and the United States Naval Service.

8

Army Sergeant Micheaux Sanders
SILVER STAR

IRAQ

I threw whatever I had at them. When we ran out of bullets,
I threw rocks.

—SERGEANT MICHEAUX SANDERS

Sergeant Micheaux Sanders describes himself as a laidback individual. Few things seem to faze him. Like, for example, the time he got shot in the shoulder by a 7.62 mm bullet fired from the AK-47 of one of Muqtada al-Sadr's militia members.

"When I got shot, I didn't really know I had gotten shot," Sergeant Sanders told us. "It wasn't until after the first phase of the battle that I looked down at my arm and noticed it was bleeding. I told another tank commander in my platoon, 'I think I got shot.' I could feel my arm hurting just a little bit, so I looked at my shirt and saw that there was a hole in it. It was my left arm, but I'm right-handed. I didn't feel it going in at all. We got to Camp War Eagle, and they all started panicking. They applied a field dressing and found a medic. They tried to get me to stay at Camp War Eagle, but I told them I didn't want to stay; I was mad I'd gotten shot and needed to get back out there. I told them, 'Give me a Band-Aid and I'll be okay.' "

Then-Specialist Micheaux Sanders speaks about the experience as though the bullet wound had been a minor scrap. But it wasn't. The enemy bullet had sliced straight through his shoulder and out the other side. Still, to the then-nineteen-year-old from Goldsboro, North Carolina, the injury seemed minor compared to the hellish scene his Quick Reaction Force tank crew and two others from C Company, Second Battalion, Thirty-seventh Armor were watching unfold around them. They had been called in to help an isolated platoon from First Cavalry patrol that had become ensnared in a massive ambush inside Sadr City, Iraq. The battle of April 4, 2004, would leave Sergeant Micheaux Sanders not only with a physical scar but also with the painful memory of losing brothers-in-arms as well.

April 4, 2004, was to have been a day of joy and celebration for then-Specialist Micheaux Sanders. It was his last day in-country. In just a few days he, along with roughly a third of the army's First Armored Division, had been scheduled to leave Iraq. Sanders had been in Iraq since June 2003, and his time in war had been somewhat of a baptism by fire. At only nineteen years old, Sanders deployed to Operation Iraqi Freedom straight out of army basic training. However, the 6 feet 1, 165-pound Sanders was accustomed to moving fast and overcoming obstacles. In high school, Sanders had been a track star. His best event: hurdles.

Still, it wasn't until his uncle, who currently serves in the U.S. Army, sat him down and told him about the benefits of a military career that he began to seriously consider it as a career choice. His interest in computer engineering and electronics propelled him to research his options further. Shortly thereafter, he decided to enlist.

Having scored high on his ASVAB test, he had quickly caught the eye of his superiors. Soon, he had established a reputation as a fast learner and analytical thinker. In particular, Sanders displayed a knack for using his hands and fixing things that were broken, especially electronics. But on April 4, 2004—what was to have been his last day in-country—tinkering with electronics, or anything else for that matter, was the farthest thing from his mind. Like any soldier, Specialist Sanders had begun thinking about reuniting with friends and family. In fact, he and the other members of Charlie Company had already packed up most of their equipment in preparation for leaving the theater; they were ready to go. Even the "big bullets"—the 120 mm tank rounds—usually stocked in his M1-A1 Abrams tank had been reduced to a minimum load for transport.

As the loader of his four-man tank crew, Specialist Sanders's duties included providing rear protection, air assault protection, and loading the main gun: the M-256 120mm smoothbore cannon, which Sanders says should only take a loader three seconds to accomplish. At 32 feet long and 12 feet wide and weighing 67.6 tons, the M1-A1 Abrams is capable of traveling at top speeds of 41 mph. Indeed, the close-quarters confines that a tank's commander, driver, loader, and gunner share builds a sense of unity and cohesion. That was certainly the case with Sanders's tank crew, each of whom would soon become decorated heroes.

The driver, Specialist Jason Rakes, would receive the Bronze Star with a device for valor. The gunner, Sergeant Patrick Jordan, would receive the Silver Star, as would the tank's commander, twenty-five-year-old West Point graduate First Lieutenant Christopher P. Dean, who, like Sanders, would suffer wounds to his neck and arm.

"I love being a platoon leader," said First Lieutenant Dean. "There's nothing in the world like the American soldier. Even in the face of a kill zone, they knew other soldiers out there were depending on us and not a single man second-guessed his duty."[1]

The tank commander's words more than described the soldiers' actions that day. Indeed, as Company Commander Captain John C. Moore, who in 2005 was awarded the U.S. Department of the Army's General Douglas MacArthur Leadership Award, explained, the tankers' courage under fire was nothing short of inspirational: "Specialist Micheaux Sanders and Sergeant Patrick Jordan . . . taught me that fanatical commitment to the accomplishment of the mission and the lives of their comrades is worth more than we can accurately assess."[2]

Throughout his ten-month stint in-country, Sanders had yet to see major action. But all that changed when radical Muslim cleric Muqtada al-Sadr's militia, the Mahdi Army, ignited a sixty-day uprising that would ultimately claim the lives of nineteen U.S. soldiers and wound several more.[3] Minutes after the uprising began on day one, Sergeant Micheaux Sanders was among the very first to arrive on the scene.

The call had come at around three P.M. Iraq time. It was urgent.

"We were at our campsite at Martyr's Monument in Baghdad

when we got the call. As part of the quick reaction force (QRF), they said we needed to get over to Sadr City fast. Members of First Cav [Cavalry] had been ambushed by members of what we later learned were Sadr's militia," said Sanders.

First Lieutenant Chris Dean, Sergeant Patrick Jordan, Specialist Jason Rakes, and Sanders all raced to their M1-A1 Abrams tank. Two other M1-A1 tank crews joined them. With Sanders's tank leading the way, the three tanks then sped at top speed to the scene of the ambush.

During the five- to ten-minute tank ride toward the urban warfare zone, Sergeant Sanders says the tankers had no idea what to expect. Having already turned in most of their 120mm tank rounds, when the tanks rolled into the kill zone, the soldiers were woefully low on ammunitions: "We had four drums of 7.62 machine-gun ammo; two hundred rounds of .50-cal ammo; two magazines of M-16 rifle ammo, and thirty rounds of 9mm pistol ammo."[4]

Still, even had all three tanks been armed to the hilt, no one could have anticipated the massive wall of firepower they were about to run into.

"We were the quick-reaction force, which meant we were the only ones there initially. When we got there, there was a platoon of scouts," recalls Sanders. "There were about ten army soldiers. Some of them were dead or injured. There were two blown-up Humvees. I could see the soldiers shooting from behind Humvees that had been hit by RPG. But when we rode up on the scene all I could see was the muzzle flashes and RPGs. When they [RPG] go by your head they sound like a whistle. I then saw explosions and gunshots hitting the tank. You had to just make sure you didn't get shot."

Thousands of fighters from the Mahdi Army had decided to engage multiple elements of the Second Battalion, Fifth Cavalry Regiment, First Cavalry Division in near simultaneous attacks throughout Sadr City in northern Baghdad. According to Company Commander Captain John C. Moore, twenty soldiers from Comanche Red Platoon, Second–Fifth Cavalry, had become isolated inside the northern central portion of Sadr City, but available vehicles prevented the unit's exfiltration.[5]

Sergeant Sanders says his tank crew had been surprised by the enormity of the enemy ambush because they had visited the area a few days prior. But with city buildings peering down over their eight-foot-tall M1-A1 Abrams tanks, the three tanks from Charlie Company were now trapped in a maelstrom of enemy fire. It was urbanized warfare at its worst. The enemy fighters burrowed in buildings were in some cases only one hundred feet away.

"The enemy were everywhere. It was a few thousand," said Sanders. "They were hiding in buildings, on top of roofs, everywhere. There were even kids shooting at us. They had kids getting weapons from the dead bodies and bringing them back to their parents."

With the absence of 120mm tank rounds essentially neutralizing the tanks' main guns, the commander ordered his tank crews to fight "open hatch," using their small-arms fire. The besieged First Cavalry soldiers needed cover in order to evacuate casualties. Sergeant Sanders popped up out of the left hatch hole (the loader's side) while his tank commander, First Lieutenant Dean, popped up out of the right hatch. As the soldiers emerged from the armored walls of their tanks and out into the open air, a day that had begun as one of celebration would soon morph into one of mourning.

"The air was full of smoke and fire. You could smell all the carbon from the shooting," remembers Sanders.

His eyes darted twenty feet from his tank to a motioning figure. It was Commander Captain John C. Moore. Moore's hand signals indicated he wanted Sanders to leave his tank and switch places with him. Captain Moore's radio was down, and as the leader it was essential that he maintain communications to give clear commands. Sanders, the electronics whiz, and his commander pushed up and out from their hatches and dashed the twenty feet fully exposed. Asked how he felt at that moment, Sanders said he didn't have time to feel much of anything.

"When I got inside the other tank I started doing everything I knew how to do with the radios. It took me about ten or fifteen minutes to get them back up and working. Our tank got hit a few times by RPG and bullets. But in an M1-A1, you don't really feel it. You just sort of feel a ding."

Even so, the M1-A1 Abrams armored walls were of little use now. Fighting open hatch would require that the soldiers be exposed from the torso up. Facing a city full of buildings brimming with over a thousand insurgents, the three tank crews stood in their hatches and gave everything they had. Sanders fired the 240 loader machine gun from the left side of the tank. Once depleted, he grabbed his M-4 Carbine. Everywhere the soldiers looked was a target.

"I threw whatever I had at them," said Sanders. "When we ran out of bullets, I threw rocks."

Meanwhile the militia fighters concentrated on alleyways, shop windows, and low roofs of one-story buildings throughout the assault. The enemy displayed tactical patience and waited until the U.S. soldiers were within 150 meters to fire. The tanks fired .50-caliber rounds or coax fire as they moved into the Meredi market. Thick with shop stands, kiosks, and commercial stands that hugged the streets, the structures provided the enemy with cover and concealment. Worse, the streets of the war zone had been converted into a maze of burning blockades. The enemy had dragged large metal objects like air conditioners and refrigerators into the path the tanks were to take. All the while, the soldiers took a constant and intense hail of enemy fire.[6]

Early on during the three-hour fight, Sergeant Sanders looked down at his cammies and noticed what appeared to be a hole. That's when he told First Lieutenant Dean that he thought he might have been hit near his shoulder socket. "The medics all kept trying to signal that they wanted to come to my aid in the middle of the battle, but I didn't want them to come out there for something like that, so I waved them off." When his tank went around the city to regroup with the other tanks from his platoon, Sanders was taken to Camp War Eagle to be examined. After telling the medics to "give me a Band-Aid and I'll be okay," he reentered the battlefield and rejoined the fight. By then, another company had showed up and re-supplied his tank and others with the desperately needed 120mm "big bullets."

"I remember during the fight being about twenty feet behind the tank that contained Sergeant Michael Mitchell, a tank mechanic. At the time we didn't know he had been shot, but we found out soon after that. Sergeant Mitchell had been shot in the head and killed," said Sanders.

Sergeant Mitchell, twenty-five, who was posthumously awarded the Bronze Star, had plans to marry his fiancée, Bianca Liebl, whom he had met while stationed in Germany. The soldier's father, Bill Mitchell, had fought in the Vietnam War. Opposed to Operation Iraq Freedom from the outset, following his son's death Bill Mitchell gained considerable media coverage after appearing on the pages of the *New York Times* and several other major newspapers and television stations.[7] He also joined with Cindy Sheehan and other antiwar activists to publicize his opposition to the war. In an interview with Paul Rockwell, Bill Mitchell expressed his views about his son's valor as well as his strong opposition to the war:

> He volunteered for a dangerous mission, risked his life to save his buddies. I believe that the actions on the day he died make him a hero. But in the broader scheme of things, I do not think the war is a war of self-defense. I am having a major problem with being OK with his death under the circumstances. And I don't really believe that Iraq or the world or the lives of his family and friends are better due to his death . . . Mike was killed by the very people he liberated. That's insane . . . I refuse to let my son die quietly for an unjust war. I was against the war before it began. I was semi-politically active. Now Mike's memory pushes me. I have raised the level of my activism. Now that my son will never come home, I am more firmly against the war than ever. A fire has been lit within me and unfortunately, the path of my life has been altered. I feel that I must put myself out there and do whatever I can to see that no

other parent learns of the pain that comes with losing a child to war.[8]

Another person who shares in Bill Mitchell's suffering and grief over the loss of his son is Sergeant Micheaux Sanders: "I don't like the memories. I don't think about it, about losing friends. I sometimes have bad dreams and flashbacks," said Sanders.

The night of Sergeant Mitchell's death, Sergeant Sanders didn't get back to Camp Martyr until two A.M. He hadn't eaten the entire day. "When I got back that night, I was really tired. The medics gave me Percocets for the pain, but I was too tired to listen to what they were saying while they were taking pictures of my arm. So I went to sleep. I got four hours of sleep that night. Then got back out there on the tanks."

The events of April 4, 2004, were the first day in what became a sixty-day Shiite uprising that resulted in an estimated fifteen hundred insurgents killed. Over that period, nineteen U.S. soldiers were killed in combat as more than five thousand soldiers from the First Armored Division waged the most sustained urban combat operation yet waged at that point in the war.[9]

Micheaux Sanders left Iraq July 17, 2004. Shortly after returning home he was promoted to sergeant. Today he says his arm feels like normal. A newlywed husband, Sergeant Sanders and his wife now live in Fort Worth, Texas. In June 2008 he will have fulfilled his military commitment. Sanders says he has yet to decide whether he will remain career military or will reenter civilian life. Currently, he serves as a supply sergeant and says that there is a possibility he may be redeployed to

U.S. Marine Capt. Brian Chontosh (right) receives the Navy Cross from Gen. Michael W. Hagee. *(Photograph by Cpl. Jeremy M. Vought / Courtesy of U.S. Marine Corps)*

U.S. Marine Cpls. Armand McCormick (left) and Robert Kerman (center) receiving their Silver Stars from General Hagee *(Photograph by Cpl. Jeremy M. Vought / Courtesy of U.S. Marine Corps)*

U.S. Marine Sgt. Marco Martínez, Navy Cross, Iraq
(Courtesy of Marco Martínez)

U.S. Air Force Master Sgt. William "Calvin" Markham (center)
in Afghanistan with six Afghani comrades. Markham was awarded
the first Silver Star in the War on Terror. *(Courtesy of U.S. Air Force)*

Army Master Sgt. Patrick Quinn,
Silver Star, Iraq *(Courtesy of U.S. Army)*

Marine 1st Sgt. Justin LeHew, Navy Cross, Iraq
(Photograph by Cpl. Daniel J. Fosco / Courtesy of U.S. Marine Corps)

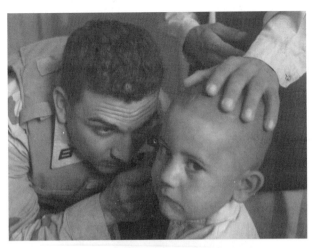

Navy Hospital Corpsman, 3rd Class, Luis Fonseca, Jr.,
Navy Cross, Iraq *(Courtesy of U.S. Navy)*

Army Sgt. Micheaux Sanders,
Silver Star, Iraq
(Courtesy of U.S. Army)

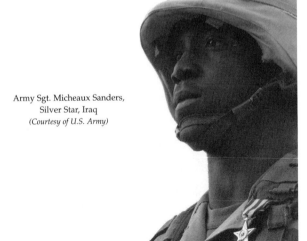

Army National Guard Sgt. Leigh Ann Hester, the first woman to receive a Silver Star for combat, standing over a captured weapons cache collected after her squad repelled an insurgent attack in Baghdad
(Courtesy of U.S. Army)

From left: Staff Sgt. Timothy Nein, awarded the Silver Star; Sgt. Leigh Ann Hester, awarded the Silver Star; Spc. Jason Mike, awarded the Silver Star; also seen here are Spc. Casey Cooper, awarded the Bronze Star Medal with Valor device; Sgt. Dustin Morris, awarded the Army Commendation Medal with Valor device; and Spc. Jesse Ordunez, awarded the Army Commendation Medal with Valor device.
(Courtesy of U.S. Army)

Amy Morel, wife of Marine Capt. Brent L. Morel, stares into the bronze statue of her husband. Amy received the Navy Cross on behalf of Brent for his valor in actions that led to his death on April 7, 2004, in Fallujah, Iraq. *(Photograph by Lance Cpl. Miguel A. Carrasco, Jr. / Courtesy of U.S. Marine Corps)*

Marine Sgt. William Copeland III, Navy Cross, Iraq *(Photograph by Lance Cpl. Joseph L. DiGirolamo / Courtesy of U.S. Marine Corps)*

Army Sfc. Paul Ray Smith, who was issued the U.S. military's highest honor, the Congressional Medal of Honor, posthumously for his heroism in Iraq *(Courtesy of U.S. Army)*

President George W. Bush with Paul Ray Smith's family during the Congressional Medal of Honor ceremony. (From left) Smith's stepdaughter, Jessica, 18; wife, Birgit; and son, David, 11. *(Courtesy of U.S. Army)*

Army Lt. Col. Mark Mitchell, Distinguished Service Cross, Afghanistan *(Courtesy of U.S. Army)*

Marine Sgt. Rafael Peralta, Purple Heart recipient and nominated for the Congressional Medal of Honor for heroic actions that cost him his life in Iraq *(Courtesy of U.S. Marine Corps)*

Commander Robert D. Delis gives a cross to Rosa Maria Peralta after the body of her son, Sgt. Rafael Peralta, was laid to rest. *(Photograph by Cpl. Edward R. Guevara, Jr. / Courtesy of U.S. Marine Corps)*

Iraq. If so, Sergeant Sanders says that if he ever finds himself wounded again in battle there is definitely one thing he will do differently: "When I got shot, I didn't tell my Mom at first. I started to think about it, and I said to myself, 'Now, you're going to get in trouble if you don't tell her.' So one day I just called her at work and said, 'Mama, I got shot and I'm fine.' It had been about a month since it had happened. She got mad at me for not having told her sooner."

At only twenty-one, Sergeant Sanders has already developed a philosophy of leadership, his words bearing the patina of experience: "Leaders are made. When they are put into certain situations, they know how to react to it. It makes them become a leader. During the fight you have to be a team or you won't make it. Everyone treats everyone the same."

An avid rap fan (Notorious B.I.G. and Pastor Troy are two of his favorites) and reader of books, Sergeant Sanders says that many young people today remain uninformed about foreign policy and world events because they don't read. While his experiences in battle undoubtedly helped shape his world-view, one thing that remains unchanged is his "low-profile" nature. During the medal ceremony in Germany, where he and his crewmates received their medals, crowds and reporters swarmed many of the medal recipients. Sanders, however, stood quietly beside his tank in an effort to avoid the spotlight and publicity. He says it made him feel out of place.

"The medal's cool, but all the fuss feels weird. I'm in the Army. This is my job."[10]

9

Army National Guard Sergeant
Leigh Ann Hester
SILVER STAR

Army National Guard Specialist Jason Mike
SILVER STAR

Army National Guard Staff Sergeant
Timothy Nein
SILVER STAR

IRAQ

My heroes don't play in the NBA and don't play in the U.S.
Open at Pinehurst. They're standing in front of me today.
These are American heroes.

—ARMY LIEUTENANT GENERAL JOHN R. VINES,
MULTINATIONAL CORPS IRAQ COMMANDING GENERAL
AT A JUNE 16, 2005, AWARDS CEREMONY

It hadn't happened since 1944.

That was the year Mary Louise Roberts—the army nurse
who defied orders to take cover when shrapnel ripped through
her surgical tent and instead rushed to the aid of "her boys" in
Anzio, Italy—was awarded the Silver Star. Yet even including

Roberts, no female GI in American history has ever received a medal for actions rendered while actively fighting an enemy of the United States. That is, not until March 20, 2005, when Army National Guard Sergeant Leigh Ann Hester took actions that would forever change U.S. military history.

"It's a great honor to receive it [Silver Star]. But I'm just another soldier here. It's all in a day's work. It's what we're here to do. We're here to protect other soldiers and convoys trying to get from one place to another," said Hester.[1]

Indeed, Sergeant Hester, twenty-three, a military police officer (MP) from Fourth Platoon, 617th Military Police Company, 503rd MP Battalion, 18th MP Brigade, is quick to point out that she wasn't the only person—male or female—engaged in the forty-five-minute firefight that took place roughly twelve miles southeast of Baghdad in the town of Salman Pak. Hester says the nine other members of her Kentucky Army National Guard squad, Raven 42, proved their bravery with equal measure when the convoy of thirty tractor-trailers they were charged with protecting was ambushed by a force of fifty Iraqi insurgents armed with automatic weapons and RPG. In so doing, these army national guard "weekend warriors" lived up to the highest traditions of the U.S. Army.

It's hard to imagine a more diverse collection of individuals than the ten soldiers who make up the military police squad known as Raven 42: Specialist Casey Cooper, Specialist William Haynes, Sergeant Leigh Ann Hester, Specialist Bryan Mack, Specialist Jason Mike, Sergeant Dustin Morris, Staff Sergeant Timothy Nein, Specialist Jesse Ordunez, Specialist

Ashley Pullen, and Sergeant Joseph Rivera. After all, where else would a manager of a Shoe Carnival, a former fullback for Jacksonville University's football team, and an employee of International Paper find themselves shoulder to shoulder in the fight of their lives? But such is the nature of today's army national guard, which draws its strength from the kaleidoscope of Americans who all sign up to serve as "weekend warriors."

The training these soldiers receive is no less rigorous than the program for those who serve full-time active duty, nor is their passion and commitment any less intense. Unlike the army reserve, which is completely controlled by the federal government and serves solely as a federal reserve to the active army, the army national guard may be controlled by either the state or the federal government, depending on the circumstance. The army guard force structure consists of combat, combat support, and combat service support units, while the army reserve force is primarily comprised of combat support and combat service support. Today, the guard consists of approximately 340,000 soldiers versus just over 200,000 in the reserves. In Iraq, roughly 40 percent of U.S. forces are national guard and reserves.

Patterned after the English militia systems, the history of the army national guard began on December 13, 1636, when the Massachusetts Bay Colony organized three militia regiments to defend against the growing threat of the Pequot Indians. At the time, all males between sixteen and sixty were obligated to own and take up arms in defense of the community. That tradition has continued throughout American history, as nineteen U.S. presidents have served in the national guard.

What has changed, of course, is the role women now play in the U.S. military. In 1994, Pentagon policy stipulated that women were not to be included in direct ground combat units smaller than brigades. This means that Special Forces (SF), infantry, and armor units, for example, are off-limits to female soldiers. However, as a *New York Times* article covering Sergeant Hester's heroic actions points out, increasingly, the counterinsurgency in Iraq has blurred the traditional battlefield boundaries, thus putting troops in support units, such as the military police, in direct combat. With fifteen thousand female troops currently in Iraq, and thirty-five servicewomen having been killed in-country, it is clear that the service and sacrifice of female soldiers remain significant.[2]

Sergeant Leigh Ann Hester is one of the fifteen thousand female soldiers waging the War on Terror. She was born in Bowling Green, Kentucky, and then later moved to Nashville, Tennessee. Standing a mere five feet four, Hester's southern roots can be heard in the twang in her voice. Back in Nashville, Tennessee, Hester is the manager of a Shoe Carnival shoe store. A member of the national guard since April 2001, she says she has always considered herself a "tomboy." And gauging from her John Wayne–like strut, she means it. But the emphasis on her gender, and the "GI Jane" rhetoric that surrounds her, she says, misses the broader point.

"It really doesn't have anything to do with being a female. . . . Your training kicks in and the soldier kicks in. It's your life or theirs. . . . You've got a job to do—protecting yourself and your fellow comrades," said Hester.[3]

While Hester steers clear of the larger debate over Pentagon policy that prevents female soldiers from engaging in full combat roles alongside their male counterparts, she feels that women can and are holding their own: "Being in the MPs, we're out there every day doing the same jobs as men. I'm perfectly happy being a military police officer."[4]

Hester's fellow Silver Star recipient and Raven 42 teammate, Specialist Jason Mike, the twenty-two-year old, 250-pound brick wall of a man and former Jacksonville University fullback, agrees. Hester, he says, is "One of a kind . . . I think she was all about work and no play." As Mike sees it, Hester's Silver Star "is good for all women in the armed forces."[5]

Standing side by side, Mike and Hester are quite a contrast. But their commitment to one another and their fellow guardsmen are identical. Mike, an army brat and self-described entrepreneur who now works in real estate and the restaurant industry, says he joined the guard shortly after the September 11 terrorist attacks. Eventually, Specialist Mike, who lives in Radcliffe, Kentucky, says he would like to join the active-duty army and fly Black Hawk helicopters.

The man leading Hester and Mike was Raven 42's squad leader, Staff Sergeant Timothy Nein, thirty-six, of Henryville, Indiana. He has worked for International Paper for fifteen years and is described as a "lanky family man with two young sons."[6] At the time of his actions, Nein was on his second deployment to Iraq. Asked about his heroic actions, the deferential leader is quick to share credit with those whom he leads: "It's due to their [Hester, Mike, and the other seven members of Raven 42] dedication and their ability to stay there and back me up that we were able to do what we did that day."[7]

What the ten members of Raven 42 "did that day" during their forty-five-minute firefight against fifty Iraqi insurgents was save each others' lives and the lives of many in the convoy of thirty tractor-trailers by killing twenty-seven insurgents, wounding six, and capturing one.

On March 20, 2005, the ten members of Raven 42 rolled along the dusty roads of Salman Pak, about twelve miles southeast of Baghdad. Back home in Kentucky, the 617th Military Police Company, to which Raven 42 belongs, is tasked with providing garrison security and support throughout the state and to provide crowd control at events, such as the Kentucky Derby. But in Iraq, the company's tasks were different, decidedly so. Their primary job involved protecting vehicle convoys and patrolling the supply routes in and out of Baghdad. And as the *Washington Post* reports, this work proved extremely dangerous. Since November, Raven 42 had encountered an approximate thirty roadside bombs, two-thirds of which were detonated near the squad.[8]

"We're infantry with badges, is the way I like to refer to it," said Staff Sergeant Timothy Nein.[9]

On this particular day, Raven 42 rode in three armored Humvees. In the first vehicle, Squad Leader Nein rode in the passenger's seat, Specialist Casey Cooper was in the turret on the .50-caliber, and Sergeant Dustin Morris was at the wheel. Behind them, the second Humvee was driven by Specialist Ashley Pullen, Sergeant Leigh Ann Hester rode shotgun, and Specialist Jesse Ordunez manned the gun. Bringing up the rear was the third Humvee. Specialist Bryan Mack drove, Sergeant Joseph Rivera rode in the passenger's seat, Specialist William Hayes was at the gun, and army medic, Specialist Jason Mike, rode in the back.

As the three Humvees made their way along the supply route, they were passed by a half-mile-long convoy of roughly thirty supply vehicles, many of which were eighteen-wheelers, loaded with supplies for coalition forces. Staff Sergeant Timothy Nein, noticing the size of the convoy, thought it best that Raven 42 shadow the convoy to assure safe passage through the heavily traveled supply route. So, trailing the last vehicle in the convoy, Nein's Humvee led the other two MP Humvees.

Up ahead, on the right side of the road was an orchard that obscured a road that ran perpendicular to the main highway. But for the most part, the surrounding terrain was about what one might expect: the typical mix of sand, shrubs, and crusty craggy earth. Within minutes, the docile landscape morphed into one of extreme violence.

"We observed the convoy we were trailing starting to make erratic movements," remembers Staff Sergeant Nein. "We saw a lot of dust being kicked up by the convoy vehicles, as if they were being engaged by an improvised explosive device (IED) or an ambush, so we knew something was wrong." That's when Specialist Casey Cooper, still sitting in the gunner's turret, screamed, "They're taking fire! Go! Go!" Moving toward the sound of gunfire, Sergeant Dustin Morris mashed the gas and jerked around the line of convoy vehicles. Humvees two and three followed in tow. "Flank 'em down the road!" Nein yelled.[10]

The idea was to race parallel to the long row of convoy vehicles until Raven 42 located the kill zone and then jut themselves between the coalition vehicles and the Iraqi fighters in order to draw fire away from the convoy and onto themselves.

The 617th company commander, Captain Todd M. Linder, says he has reviewed the decisions his soldiers made hundreds of times and says their situational awareness and combat leadership were peerless.

"They did exactly what they were supposed to do when supporting a convoy in that situation. What their mission was in shadowing that convoy was to provide support in the event of an attack. What they were supposed to do was place themselves in between the attacking force and the convoy. This would allow the convoy to escape the kill zone while they returned suppressive fire and ultimately defeated the enemy. That was exactly what they did."[11]

Whizzing past the row of convoy, the vehicles resembled a blurry wall. In Humvee number two, Sergeant Leigh Ann Hester could see smoke pluming ahead in the distance. This wasn't one or two random enemy fighters. This was big. This was bad.

Top military blog website BlackFive.net, which obtained clearance to republish the after action report (AAR) from Raven 42's firefight, notes that army doctrine and training teach that, when ambushed, soldiers are to move directly into the ambush, never away; always into it. Doing so, however, requires that soldiers be highly trained and disciplined. And that's exactly what Raven 42 did. Following the command of their NCOs, they engaged the enemy head on.

"We moved to contact," said Nein. "We got the vehicles on the contact side, in between the convoy and the insurgents. As we got up on that side of the road, we realized through previous reconnaissance of the area that there was a road that paralleled the field going south," said Nein.[12]

Nein's driver found a gap in the row of eighteen-wheelers and sped through the hole and into the center of the kill zone. With RPG and small-arms fire crisscrossing each other in the air, the Humvees took a fast right turn onto the side road that the orchard had largely obscured from view.

No sooner had they turned onto the road than they saw seven insurgent vehicles—BMWs, Caprices, Opel sedans—all lined up in a perfect row. Each had been staged and ready. To their amazement, the enemy insurgent force numbered between forty and fifty fighters.[13]

"Doors open, trunks open; ready for a quick escape," recalls Squad Leader Nein. "Once we turned down that road, the insurgents didn't have a choice but to stay and fight. We had just cut off their escape route. As we came on the scene, the insurgents' fire all shifted. They realized who they needed to fire on. They quickly shifted all fire from the transportation convoy to us. As soon as we cut back to get in between the convoy and the insurgents, the windshield of my driver [Morris] took two direct hits. The bullets failed to defeat the armored glass."[14]

But Staff Sergeant Nein's Humvee would not be immune from taking fire for long. His gunner, Specialist Casey Cooper, remained exposed. "I saw smoke and a black dot," remembers Cooper. "All I had time to say was 'Oh crap.' "[15]

An RPG slammed into the Humvee, just above the rear passenger door, just inches from where Cooper sat in the turret. Cooper's body fell inside the vehicle and lay motionless.

"Coop, are you okay?" Nein screamed.

No response.

"Believing he was dead, I began to climb up on top of him

to get up on the weapon." But that's when Cooper, who had been temporarily knocked unconscious by shrapnel that had peppered the area around his right eye and hand, popped back up and regained consciousness. "I'm okay, I'm okay," said Cooper, before hopping back up into the turret to man the .50-caliber.[16]

Meanwhile, Sergeant Hester, still behind the now-hit vehicle, had her eyes locked on Nein's Humvee. "Nein's vehicle took a direct hit with an RPG as soon as we made that turn," said Hester. "I hear it hit, saw the smoke, but we kept pushing on. I saw Staff Sergeant Nein jump out of the truck. As soon as I saw him jump out, I was right there. On the right-hand side was a berm. They [enemy fighters] were still shooting at us from there and from down in a trench line. So we returned fire. I think I shot off three M203 [grenade launcher] rounds, and I don't know how many M-4 [assault rifle] rounds I shot. I know I hit one of the RPK [Russian-made light machine gun] gunners."[17]

Both Hester and Nein's vehicles were now being engaged by insurgents firing RPK rounds at them from somewhere inside the orchard. The enemy fighters, wearing civilian clothes and masks, were armed with AK-47s, RPG, and RPK machine guns. Outnumbered five to one, the MPs were now in a hurricane of fire. At one point, Specialist Jason Mike, the medic, remembers seeing between sixteen and twenty insurgents lining a trench parallel to the main road and dozens more firing from within the orchard. Later, American forces reported that they had found handcuffs on some of the insurgents, a sign that the enemy fighters had planned to take hostages.[18]

"We were taking fire everywhere," said Hester. "I just remember hearing the pings of the bullets going by me and hitting the ground beside me."[19]

Nein, Hester, and Morris were now out on foot and gathered together behind a four-foot berm. Nein locked in on an enemy peeking his head out from behind a tree. The moment the enemy popped his head out from behind the tree, Nein squeezed the trigger and landed a direct hit to the insurgent's head. Hester, meanwhile, had honed in on an enemy fighter spraying his RPK machine gun. "I just put that little dot on him ["aim point"] and squeezed the trigger. It hit him and he fell down. I was like, 'Whoa, I just killed somebody.' Before that first one, it was almost like it wasn't real. Now it was for real."[20] Sergeant Hester then swiveled her torso, aimed at another enemy shooter, and dropped him as well.

With Staff Sergeant Nein and Sergeant Hester busy taking down shooters, Army Medic Jason Mike, the former college fullback, had his hands full tending to his wounded comrades. Mack and Rivera had both been hit. The football-player-turned-medic bandaged both soldiers up before dragging them both under the Humvee to shield them from enemy fire. But with Mack and Rivera out of the equation, Mike knew they needed more fire power—much more. He propped up the gunner's Squad Automatic Weapon (SAW) on the Humvee and began firing it with his right hand. "I took the M-4 in my left hand to have fire on our backside because we were getting fire on our backside at this time. I began firing those two weapons simultaneously."[21]

In the official after action report (AAR), Specialist Jason Mike would later explain that being thrown into the thick of the fight instead of tending to his traditional medical duties had been made easier by the fact that his NCOs had, just a week prior, made him learn how to fire the very weapons he used during the fight, weapons he thought he would never use as a medic.

"In my mind," remembers Mike, "I'm saying, 'I'm not going to be on Al Jazeera begging for my life!' That motivated me to stay in the fight."[22]

Still, even as Mike was busy firing weapons with both hands in opposite directions, insurgents continued to fire on Raven 42's position. Much of the fire was coming from four insurgents burrowed in a trench on the other side of the berm behind which Staff Sergeant Nein and Sergeant Hester were positioned. That's when the two leaders decided it was up to them to neutralize the threat and provide cover to evacuate the wounded.

"It was crazy, adrenaline pumping," said Sergeant Hester. "You didn't have time to think about everything that was going on. It was kill or be killed."[23]

The tandem leaders then rolled up and over the berm and into the trench. The enemy shooters were just thirty yards away and were spaced five yards apart. Their heads would pop up like gophers, they would spray their AK-47s at Nein and Hester, and then pop back down in the crusty terrain. But the soldiers pressed forward and laid down fire. Hester then spied an insurgent about fifteen yards away. She unpinned a grenade and hurled it at him before hugging the ground. She looked up to the sight of the enemy slumping to the ground. Minutes later, Nein threw a grenade—one of a total four—and took out another insurgent. With that, the trench fell silent.

Backup squads from the 617th arrived to help assess the battlefield. Three of Raven 42's ten members were badly injured, but all lived. The same, of course, could not be said for the insurgents who had mounted the ambush on the convoy. Strewn throughout the trench and orchard were the bodies of twenty-seven dead insurgents, six wounded enemy, and one captured fighter. The AAR lists the following seized cache of weapons: 22 AK-47s, 6 RPG launchers with 16 rockets, 13 RPK machine guns, 3 PKM machine guns, 40 hand grenades, 123 fully loaded 30-round AK magazines, 52 empty magazines, and 10 belts of 2,500 rounds of PK ammo.

During a June 16, 2005, awards ceremony at Camp Liberty, Iraq, Sergeant Leigh Ann Hester became the first female soldier in six decades to receive the Silver Star, and the first in U.S. military history to receive the award for actions performed in battle. Seven others from Raven 42 received medals as well. Staff Sergeant Timothy Nein and Specialist Jason Mike both received Silver Stars; Specialist Casey Cooper, Specialist William Haynes II, and Specialist Ashley Pullen all received the Bronze Star with valor device; and Sergeant Dustin Moore and Specialist Jesse Ordunez received the Army Commendation Medal with valor device.

During the awards ceremony, Lieutenant General John R. Vines, the U.S. ground commander in Iraq, began tearing up as he turned to award the soldiers standing before him. "My heroes don't play in the NBA and don't play in the U.S. Open at Pinehurst. They're standing in front of me today. These are American heroes," said Vines.[24]

Equally proud and filled with emotion were the parents of

the soldiers. "I'm overwhelmed at what she's accomplished in Iraq," Jerry Hester, Sergeant Hester's father, told reporters. "It's something to be very proud of and my wife and I are. Leigh Ann is a very good soldier. She played softball and basketball all through high school, and she's won a lot of games. But those games didn't mean nowhere near what this medal does and what she's done for her country."[25]

Indeed, what she had done for her country, according to her medal citation, "saved the lives of numerous convoy members. Her bravery is in keeping with the finest traditions of military heroism."

But for all the focus on her gender, Sergeant Leigh Ann Hester finds the whole issue largely irrelevant. As she told one CNN reporter, "We are equal in the United States Army, men and women. The only thing we are not allowed in is combat of arms, infantry, field artillery, things like that. But as MPs, we are out there every day outside of the wire sweeping for roadside bombs and dealing with insurgents. So, in my opinion, I think women do just as good a job as the men."

Despite having secured her place in history as the first women to receive the Silver Star in combat, the Shoe Carnival manager-turned-war-hero displays her sense of Southern humility with a shrug. "It's a great honor to receive it. But I'm just another soldier here."[26]

A soldier, indeed.

10

Air Force Staff Sergeant Stephen Achey
SILVER STAR

AFGHANISTAN

> I was just certain that everything from my waist down must
> have been blown off. I didn't want to look.
>
> **—STAFF SERGEANT STEPHEN ACHEY**

For most twenty-two-year-old Americans, March 2, 2002, was just another day. But for then-Senior Airman Stephen M. Achey, it would be a day that would define him. As Operation Anaconda unfolded in the Shahikot Valley of Afghanistan, the young South Carolinian would prove to himself and eighty-five army soldiers that the bond between GIs runs deeper than allegiance to one's branch or personal safety. "I was just doing my job," Staff Sergeant Achey told us. But unlike most people in their twenties, Achey's "job" involved helping protect the lives of eighty-five men.

Controversy and important disagreements still surround the execution of Operation Anaconda. But one thing everyone seems to agree upon is that the hellish battles waged in the Shahikot Valley of Afghanistan elevated the most courageous tendencies of the human spirit, whether from Navy SEALS, Army Rangers, Army Green Berets, Army infantry, or, in the case of Stephen Achey, a member of the U.S. Air Force.[1]

Achey served as a terminal attack command and control specialist (TACC). As part of the Twentieth Air Support Operations Squadron, he was attached to the U.S. Army's Tenth Mountain Division. But the circumstances Stephen Achey found himself in on that icy day in March would demand more than the duties to which he had grown accustomed, much more. His willingness to risk his own life, combined with his computerlike ability to recall and apply obscure, seldom-used technical training would mean the difference between disaster and the fulfillment of his duty.

The day began early, at three thirty A.M. Senior Airman Achey and another airman loaded into two C-47 Chinook helicopters, along with eighty-four army soldiers. There would, of course, be the normal interbranch teasing about being a "flyboy" and the like. But as a TACC, Achey's job would be to call in close air support (CAS) to provide crucial cover for the army soldiers. That wasn't the only thing that differentiated Achey from his army counterparts, however. His 125-pound pack was loaded down with heavy radio equipment and weighed almost twice that of his army counterparts. At the time of the mission, Achey weighed around 190 pounds.

"It felt like I was carrying a dead person on my back," he told us. Moreover, he and his army counterparts would be lugging their equipment through the treacherous Afghan terrain at an elevation of ten thousand feet, with temperatures hovering between an icy twenty-five to thirty degrees Fahrenheit.

By six A.M., the two C-47 Chinooks touched ground, and the forty-three men in each helicopter filed out. Five minutes into their trek south, the unit spotted two men roughly a kilometer away waving the familiar bright orange panels that indicated they were coalition soldiers. But their actions spoke otherwise. Within seconds, the two men began firing rounds in the direction of the U.S. column. When the shooting began, Achey was positioned on the far left side of the group's wedgelike formation. And that's when Achey says all hell broke loose.

RGPs and mortars began pummeling the face of the U.S. column. The soldiers and two airmen dropped to the ground, ducked behind their rucksacks, and crouched into shooting positions. Built in 1968 for use in the Vietnam War, their guns, AR-15s, were older than they were. But Achey had been a member of his high school marksman team, and the skills he'd honed during that extracurricular activity instantly became vital.

"I spotted one of the enemy who was shooting at me about 250 meters away. He would pop up, shoot, and then duck again. Each time he did I'd take a shot, but he was so quick that this went on about fifteen or twenty times. I started getting annoyed. I needed to take him out. But finally my shot found its target. I got my first kill."

There was no time for reflection, however. His closest brush with death was minutes away.

"So there I am, feeling all cool, still hiding behind my pack when this mortar comes flying through the air and lands so close to my outstretched feet that the blast flipped my body over like a somersault."

Now lying flat on his back, the young airman says that two words raced through his mind: "I'm dead." Said Achey, "Instantly, I wasn't cool anymore.

"When I realized I was still breathing, I was just certain that everything from my waist down must have been blown off. I didn't want to look."

A moment of mortal danger such as this may have seemed like an odd time for comic relief, even for the laid-back Achey, a man who loves to laugh and refuses to take himself too seriously. But a moment of levity interjected itself anyhow. "I felt the most overwhelming need to relieve myself; I had to pee *really* badly. So I figured, *Well, if you don't have a lower half anyway, what the heck!* So I began going all down my pants. And that's when I realized, *Wait a minute! Why can I feel my legs getting wet?* So I looked down. And that's when I realized that my legs were fine! I felt like a complete idiot."

The mortar rounds continued to rain down on the U.S. position. Achey raced to set up his PRC 117F multiband tactical radio. He was determined to get his guys the air support they needed. He wanted to give the "Killer Spade" call sign for Apache helicopters. Achey then realized the unthinkable: the mortar blast and enemy gunfire pinging off his pack had damaged his sole means of communication. He couldn't call for close air support.

Just when he thought things couldn't get worse, the airman wrenched his neck around to scan the surrounding terrain. He saw no one. His teammates had all moved their locations; he was alone. Then, roughly 150 to 200 meters away, Sergeant Achey spotted forty of his guys. They had all assembled in a bowl-like indentation in the ground. Without any way to communicate, Achey faced an agonizing decision. On the one hand, were he to run without firepower to cover his jaunt up the hill and into the bowl, his teammates might mistake him for the enemy and render him a victim of friendly fire.

But his other option was hardly better: He could run carrying the glaring orange panel indicating his coalition status, which would scream "target" to enemy snipers. Leaving behind everything but his vest, helmet, and rifle, the twenty-two-year-old settled on option two and broke into a full sprint carrying the orange panel. He had about two football fields' distance between him and his unit.

There was no method to how he ran, said Achey. He just ran as fast as he'd ever run in his life. Soon, he was up and over the lip of the bowllike structure now occupied by some forty GIs. Yet with the enemy fire unrelenting, the need for close air support grew dire. He went from soldier to soldier asking whether anyone had a radio he could borrow. Someone said he could use theirs. But the unit's frequency was nothing compared to his PRC 117F. That's when Staff Sergeant Achey's memory kicked into overdrive.

While stationed in Germany, the TACC remembered something that at the time had seemed like useless information. Master Sergeant Holbrooke had told him about a seldom used "guard frequency" that was to be used to locate a possible aircraft only in extreme cases of danger. "If I had normally switched over to that frequency any other time, I would have been in big trouble. But the situation warranted the decision, so I made it. I just kept hoping someone—anyone—would hear my call."

With the crack of gunfire filling the air, Achey heard a voice crackling through the radio. It was that of a P-3C Orion surveillance pilot. The pilot said he would relay the Tenth Mountain Division's situation. Help was five minutes away. Staff Sergeant Achey stressed the dire nature of the situation. The pilot assured him that help was coming but that they needed precise coordinates. With his unit only 450 meters away from the enemy, a miscalculation could result in a tragic case of fratricide.

Achey linked up with Technical Sergeant Vick McCabe. The two men began strategizing to determine the proper map coordinates to call in an air strike. But they realized that a vital piece of equipment was missing. Worse, it had been left in the rucksack that lay out in the bullet riddled terrain Achey had fled.

For most people, sprinting across an open fire zone once would have been plenty. But Staff Sergeant Achey believed that if he could just establish precise coordinates he could dramatically tilt the balance in his unit's favor.

"I found this eighteen-year-old army guy with his M-240 and told him I needed him to cover me while I ran to get the equipment. I said, 'Okay, now you're gonna cover me on five, right?' And he said, 'Yes, absolutely. I'm definitely going to cover you.' And then I pressed him. 'Okay, so when I run out there, you're going to start suppressing fire right away, isn't that right?' 'Yes, absolutely,' he said. 'I'm going to cover you.'"

Just as Achey had instructed, the countdown began: "One, two, three, four . . . FIVE!"

Achey sprang to his feet and ran at top speed for a second

time. Achey says he could hear bullets whizzing through the air and clinking off the things around him. But then he heard another noise, this one more ominous. It was the deep, drumming sound of an enemy RPK machine gun just fifty meters away, and Achey was in its sites. The gun spit a lethal chain of fire that tracked him as he ran. Somehow, Achey managed to scoop up the needed gear, turn, and race back to the bowl without being hit.

He had survived, and he now had the tools necessary to unleash his lethal skills. The Terminal Attack Controller went to work. He wanted the subsequent air strike to suppress the enemy long enough to allow his unit to reposition themselves to better ground. So Achey ordered up an impressive assortment of American airpower and told everyone to hunker down.

At approximately 6:45 A.M., the Taliban and al Qaeda forces who had ambushed the 86 Americans received 27 MK-82 bombs, each weighing 500 pounds apiece, and Joint Direct Attack Munition (JDAM) GPS-guided bombs, weighing in at 2,000 pounds apiece, all compliments of the B-52 bomber hovering some 50,000 feet in the air who had heeded Achey's call.

"It's hard to describe how loud something like that really is. You could hear crushed pieces of rock falling back to earth. When I looked up it was just a wall of fire and smoke. Then, everything went totally silent. No enemy fire, no nothing." The strike had been a success and had allowed the group to reposition itself to what it thought was more favorable ground.

But this was a battle waged on the enemy's home turf. Achey says that he and the other soldiers realized that many of the Taliban and al Qaeda fighters had simply hunkered down into tunnels and caves once the bombs had fallen. "They all started popping out of nowhere. They were everywhere."

Now under a hail of sniper fire, the U.S. forces were taking serious hits. Six soldiers were seriously injured. In fact, the enemy's accuracy was so precise that one of its RPGs made a direct hit on a U.S. soldier's slender mortar tube. "It literally clinked off the tube," said Achey.

Next, the airman ordered up call sign "White Lightning," which produced two Strike Eagles with 12 Guided Bomb Unit (GBU) laser-guided 500-pound bombs. During their attack, the Taliban and al Qaeda forces launched a surface-to-air missile. Achey followed the missile with his eyes and quickly radioed a break maneuver to the pilot. Just as the pilot had come to the unit's rescue, Achey's instinctual response had avoided serious damage and the possible loss of the aircraft and crew.

With the wounded soldiers now losing significant amounts of blood in the frigid mountain terrain, the Americans began stacking the injured side by side in a hole before covering them to keep them warm. Achey recalls that one soldier had shrapnel lodged directly between his eyes. The adrenaline surging through the injured soldier's body had made him so numb to the pain that he had not even realized he'd been injured.

Alternating between his radio and rifle, Airman Achey kept constant communications with aircraft overhead. He soon shored up a hole in the defenses and provided covering fire when two HH-60 Pave Hawk helicopters entered the area to evacuate the wounded. "Bryne [a medic] did an incredible job," Achey remembers. "In the end, we had thirty-two guys wounded to varying degrees, but not a single one died. God bless that guy, Bryne!"

As night fell, Taliban and al Qaeda fighters shot RPGs just twenty feet from one of the U.S. helicopters involved in the extraction. "That really pissed me off," said Achey. Luckily, Achey had one of his favorite aircraft, the AC-130H Spectre gunship, escort the helicopters into the zone. "I love those guys. They're the best. They won't leave you—ever." The airstrikes continued in an effort to help take out the remaining enemy positions and fighters.

One sergeant who was in the valley fighting had also been involved with the now-infamous "Black Hawk Down" nightmare in Somalia. He described the level of intense fighting as "worse than Mogadishu." Likewise, Staff Sergeant Achey remembers that there seemed to be an endless stream of Taliban and al Qaeda fighters flooding out of nooks and crannies everywhere. Without Achey's exceptional courage and situational awareness, however, the myriad aircraft that supported the soldiers during the fight could not have achieved such accuracy. It had been a team effort.

After the twenty-hour battle had finally ceased, one of the very same C-47 Chinooks that had dropped the unit off had now landed some two hundred meters away to pick up the remaining men. Exhausted and hungry, Achey recalls that they flew back to Bagram in total silence. The only thing he had eaten during the whole ordeal had been a small MRE package of chocolate pound cake. During the battle, he had offered a piece to an army lieutenant. "No thanks," the soldier replied. "I'd rather die out here than eat that stuff." But miraculously, for the miscalculations and losses involved in Operation Ana-conda, not one member of C Company, 1-87 Battalion, Tenth Mountain Division would die that day.

When the men touched down safely at Bagram Airfield, Achey says he let out a sigh of relief. "I didn't want us to have survived something like that only to then die in a helicopter crash or something."

Word spread quickly about Achey's gallantry. In a rare mo-ment of interbranch solidarity, army soldiers began hugging and thanking him. "It was really neat, because we had done it all as a team. I just felt glad to have contributed to the effort," says Achey. He was even greeted by Canadian coalition forces that had showed up to congratulate and honor his heroics.

"It was very special to have the army guys treat me as one of their own, but I was just doing my job," said Achey. "I just did what anyone in my position would have done."

*The President of the United States of America
authorized by Act of Congress July 9, 1918, has awarded
the Silver Star*

to

Stephen Achey
United States Air Force

for service as set forth in the following:

*Senior Airman Stephen M. Achey distinguished himself by
gallantry in connection with military operations against an
armed enemy of the United States at the Shahi Kot Valley,
Afghanistan, on 2 March 2002. On that date, while performing
the duties of Enlisted Terminal Attack Controller, 20th Air
Support Operations Squadron, 18th Air Support Operations
Group, Air Combat Center, Combined Forces Land Component
Commander, C Company, 1-87 Battalion, 10th Mountain
Division, for Operation ANACONDA, Airman Achey air-
assaulted into heavily defended territory and immediately began taking heavy fire. Hit and thrown, but undeterred by the
effects of a mortar round exploding within a few feet of him,
Airman Achey returned fire and called for close air support.
Unable to contact any aircraft and with his radio now destroyed, Airman Achey braved the intense enemy fire to link up
with another controller. Airman Achey contacted a reconnaissance aircraft and relayed his unit's situation to the orbiting
command and control aircraft. Airman Achey and the other
controller took cover and began deriving coordinates to attack
the enemy. Realizing a necessary piece of equipment was left in*

the line of fire and with complete disregard for his personal safety, Airman Achey boldly ran out to retrieve the equipment. Under a hail of machine gun fire, he gathered the equipment and made it back to cover. The subsequent air strike suppressed the enemy, allowing the unit to reposition to better ground. Now receiving sniper fire, Airman Achey called in a flight of fighters. During their attack, the enemy launched a surface-to-air missile; Airman Achey quickly called a break maneuver, avoiding damage and possible loss of the aircraft and crew. Alternating between radio and his rifle, Airman Achey shored up a hole in the defenses and provided covering fire for the removal of the wounded. During this action, Airman Achey shot and killed three enemy soldiers. Throughout the battle, Airman Achey repeatedly placed himself at risk to assist the wounded. As night fell, Airman Achey orchestrated a gunship and fighter attack that destroyed numerous enemy positions and facilitated the extraction of the wounded. His courageous and aggressive acts against a determined enemy vowing to fight to the death directly affected the outcome of the battle. By his gallantry and devotion to duty, Airman Achey has reflected great credit upon himself and the United States Air Force.

11

Marine Captain Brent Morel
NAVY CROSS

Marine Sergeant Willie Copeland III
NAVY CROSS

IRAQ

Son, this is my first Christmas without you in 28 years. Today I am extremely jealous of my God. He knew you before you were born and let me borrow you for a while. How my heart aches for you. The other morning I awoke at 3 am to someone crying. It was me crying in my sleep.

—MIKE MOREL, FATHER OF CAPTAIN BRENT MOREL

On May 21, 2005, Amy Morel stood at the Marine Corps Reserve Center in Memphis, Tennessee, and stared at the bronze statue of her husband, Captain Brent L. Morel. It looked so life-like, so much like she had remembered him looking the last day she kissed him good-bye. Captain Morel's mother, Molly Morel, agreed: "The statue looked so real," his mother said. "Right down to the scar he got while he was in boot camp."[1]

Fighting back tears, Mike Morel, Brent's father, gently placed his hand on the left shoulder of the bust. It had been just over a year since the life-altering knock at their door in the tiny town of McKenzie, Tennessee.

"There was a knock at the door at three A.M. I opened it, looked at the three marines standing in front of me, and said, 'You're going to tell me my son is dead,' and they said, 'Yes, sir.' I asked the men was he in the front? They answered yes. I always knew that's where he would be."[2]

But standing there at the ceremony peering through her blonde tresses at the Navy Cross resting in its display box, Amy Morel found comfort in the preservation of her husband's legacy. "Although I would rather have him receive the award in person, I am glad to see that his brave actions did not go unnoticed."[3]

Also present at the ceremony that day was Sergeant Willie L. Copeland III, twenty-six, from Smithfield, Utah. Copeland was the marine who had a month earlier received the Navy Cross for having risked his life trying to save Captain Morel's.

"My last memories of [Captain Morel] will always be as a marine who led a team to fight in the direction of the bullets," said Sergeant Copeland. "That was the type of marine Morel was—he led from the front. He was a personal mentor of mine, so I was constantly trying to obtain knowledge from him any way I could. No medal or award can make up for the loss of a good marine, but as a recon marine [Captain Morel] knew that his life was on the line every day—and he was always proud of it."[4]

As the commander for Second Platoon, Bravo Company, First Reconnaissance Battalion, First Marine Division, First Marine Expeditionary Force, Captain Morel, twenty-seven, was charged with leading the elite force of men specially trained as "recon" marines. Similar to navy SEALs and army rangers, reconnaissance marines master a host of specialized skills and provide surveillance, clandestine operations, and support the Marine Air Ground Task Force (MAGTF), even conducting raids and hostage rescues.

In 1999, Morel graduated from the University of Tennessee–Martin with a degree in history before he decided to enlist in the marines. His marine brothers and family describe him as the type of individual who refused to tell others to do things he was unwilling to do himself; he believed in the power of example, in putting others before self. For example, one day while speaking to the father of one of his son's men, Mike Morel was surprised to learn that while in Iraq each marine was allotted a certain number of telephone minutes to call loved ones back home. "I told this other father that Brent doesn't call home much, and he said that's because Brent was giving his minutes to his men so they could speak with their loved ones a little longer."[5]

It was that same sense of dedication—of *semper fidelis*—that motivated Captain Morel on April 7, 2004, in the Al Anbar province to confront the forty- to sixty-insurgent ambush head on—just as marines are trained to do—when his fifteen-vehicle convoy came under assault. And, just as he'd witnessed his mentor do, it was this same sense of self-sacrifice and commitment that compelled Sergeant Willie Copeland to use his body as a shield to try to save his captain's life.

Al Anbar Province is Iraq's largest province. Bordering Syria, it contains the once insurgent-infested city of Fallujah and the so-called Sunni Triangle, a hotbed of anti-American hostility.

On April 7, 2004, Captain Brent L. Morel, the lean, redheaded leader of Second Platoon, Bravo Company, First Recon Battalion understood that driving a column of vehicles near Fallujah was not without its risks. Of the fifteen vehicles in the convoy, Captain Morel made sure that the first five Humvees in the column belonged to his recon platoon. Morel's Humvee was second in line.

The road the marines rolled along was ripe for ambush. The ten-foot-tall berms, irrigation ditches, and culverts alongside the Euphrates River provided myriad concealed positions from which to establish a kill zone and launch an attack. When an RPG arced over a berm some one hundred meters away and smacked into Corporal Eddie Wright's mounted machine gun and left him without both of his hands, there was really no way to know for certain from which direction(s) the ambush was coming.[6]

"Stop and dismount!" Morel yelled.

Were it possible to have hit Pause and Freeze at that moment, one would have realized that it was at that instant that each marine's razor-sharp training took control. In a flash the endless and exhausting gauntlet of drills and training exercises morphed into instinct. It was the moment when the things humans are hardwired to do in an instance of mortal danger—namely, flee and run—were subsumed and overridden by dedication to the mission and one's brothers.

"Nothing's natural about running into bullets," said Sergeant Copeland. "I was only worried about my marines and their safety."[7]

Copeland's wife, Marine Sergeant Danielle E. Copeland, twenty-four from Pasadena, Texas, says that it was her husband's preparation and conditioning that made his following of Captain Morel's orders and his personal leadership automatic: "He [Copeland] trained for battle 24/7. I knew what he did was all instinct, and I'm very proud of him," his wife said.

After Morel issued the dismount command he then ordered the last two platoon vehicles, both of which were still outside the kill zone, to establish flanking positions. The RPG that had blown off the hands of the unflappable, six feet two, Corporal Eddie Wright was the domino that set off a chain reaction of enemy fire. Mortar rounds, RPG, and a hail of assorted gunfire cracked from the weapons of the forty to sixty hidden insurgents.

"I opened my eyes and looked at my hands and I saw they were both blown off," said Wright. "I remember thinking, 'Damn, both of them?'"[8]

Looking at Wright's gruesome injuries, junior marines began "freaking out," but not Wright. As his citation for the Bronze Star with valor device states, "Understanding the severity of his own injuries, he calmly instructed others on how to remove the radio, call for support, and render first aid. He also pointed out enemy machine-gun emplacements to his fellow marines, assisting in the demise of twenty-six enemies killed in action." Later, while in physical therapy, Wright said, "I'm just glad I'm alive. I don't think I was dealt a bad hand at all. It's nobody's fault this happened to me. War is war. . . . I think the marine corps will give me a fair chance. I just need to demonstrate I can do it [continue serving]. If I could stay in my battalion that would be great. I'd trade that medal for a chance to go back there."[9]

Meanwhile, as Wright was directing the administration of his own first aid, Captain Morel had sprung into a full sprint across the open field toward the enemy berms. A mortar round crashed into Sergeant Copeland's Humvee. That's when Copeland led his five-man team through a barrage of enemy fire and into the open field to catch up to Morel. Copeland and the others laid down cover fire for their platoon leader, who had now climbed up a ten-foot berm to maneuver into a firing position. The five marines finally caught up to Morel, and it was at this point that Morel decided to lead his men through a muddy, chest-deep canal with a sinkhole bottom. They were on offense. He wanted to get closer to the enemy. Once they had waded across, only one berm separated the marines from the nest of enemy fighters. Morel looked at his marines.[10]

"Cover me. We're assaulting through," he said.

"You want to assault through?" asked Sergeant Dan Lalota.

"Yes."

"Roger that."[11]

Along the charge, they had already eliminated ten insurgents at close range, but Morel intended to finish the job. That was all his marines needed to hear. As was his custom, Captain Morel led the way. "Brent never asked anyone to do anything that he wouldn't do himself," said Morel's father. "He was the first in line. He didn't lead from the back."[12]

Just as Captain Morel got over the berm, he turned to yell back to his marines. As he did, an enemy bullet sliced through the air, went straight through his left arm, and entered his body through his armpit.[13] Morel was down.

The body of the man Sergeant Willie Copeland considered his mentor now lay on the battlefield. Copeland, mimicking his captain's leadership style, decided to lead by example. Not wanting the others to endanger themselves further, Copeland signaled for the other marines to remain in covered positions. He then rushed to Morel's aid. When he got there, Captain Morel was still conscious. Copeland tore off Morel's gear and vest and pressed his hands against Captain Morel's wounds to try and staunch the bleeding. He then tied a bandage around his chest.

"Everybody in that platoon was heavily engaged in close combat," said Colonel Rory Talkington, the marine who recommended Copeland for the Navy Cross. "The fact that Sergeant Copeland was not hit was just miraculous."

Copeland refused to leave Morel's side. For fifteen minutes he stayed with his injured captain until an armored Humvee arrived. When Morel eventually arrived at the combat hospital he was officially pronounced dead.[14]

The Navy Cross awards ceremony for Sergeant Willie Copeland III took place April 21, 2005, at the Camp Del Mar Boat Basin in California. While the mood was somewhat different from that at the ceremony to honor Captain Brent Morel, the esprit de corps on which the U.S. Marine Corps prides itself was on full display, something that would have undoubtedly pleased Captain Morel. A throng of over two hundred marines, friends, and family members had assembled for the event. The turnout overwhelmed the humble Copeland. After pinning the Navy Cross—one of only ten awarded in the War on Terror thus far—to Copeland's chest, Assistant Secretary of the Navy Richard Greco spoke.

"Charity comes from the Latin word *caritas*," said Greco.

"The direct translation comes from *caro,* which means "flesh." True love, true charity is actually defined as the "giving of flesh." There is no greater act of individual charity that a person can do than to lay down his life for love."[15]

One of those in attendance at the ceremony was Sergeant Copeland's mother, Robyn Copeland. "You don't expect him to come home and get that kind of award. However, I was very proud of him before the award," she said.[16]

It was the same pride the Morel family felt for their beloved Brent. Yet their pride had been tinged with pain. Brent and Amy had goals they wanted to achieve together. Nothing extravagant. But they had been saving up to build a home and begin having children. They had hoped to one day buy a plot of land near his parents, Mike and Molly, back in McKenzie, Tennessee, so Brent could be close to his favorite hunting buddy—his father.

For Mike Morel, the path toward healing continues. But on June 26, 2004, Mike Morel found a shimmer of encouragement and solace while surfing the Internet one evening. That's when he stumbled upon an online memorial that Tim Rivera, a twenty-three-year-old mail carrier, had created with his own money to give families, friends, and citizens a way to honor the legacy of America's fallen heroes. From time to time over the course of a year, Morel would add his own thoughts to the running string of comments from individuals who wanted to honor his son's sacrifice.

On what would have been Captain Morel's twenty-eighth birthday, his father wrote "Today he [Brent] spends his first birthday with Jesus. Happy Birthday son." On the eight-month anniversary of his son's death, Mike Morel wrote that he had talked with President Bush about his son as well as members of his platoon. "It was nice to have the President show his concern," wrote Captain Morel's father. "He [Bush] was very genuine to us and the meeting was private." And on Christmas Eve, the first in twenty-eight years without his son, Mike Morel explained his inability to sleep: "How my heart aches for you. The other morning I awoke at 3 am to someone crying. It was me crying in my sleep."[17]

As for Amy Morel, the bronze life-size bust of her hero husband now on display inside the University of Tennessee at Martin library represents a sort of living memorial of its own. "The library is where me and my husband met," said Amy. "It is only fitting that his statue be kept there to inspire those who pass by it. He was a great man."[18]

OFFICIAL NAVY CROSS CITATION

The President of the United States
takes pleasure in presenting
the Navy Cross
to

Brent Morel
United States Marine Corps

for service as set forth in the following:

The Navy Cross is awarded to Captain Brent Morel, United States Marine Corps, for extraordinary heroism as Platoon Commander, 2d Platoon, Company B, 1st Reconnaissance Battalion, 1st Marine Division, I Marine Expeditionary Force, U.S. Marine Corps Forces, Central Command in support of Operation IRAQI FREEDOM on 7 April 2004. Captain Morel's platoon escorted a convoy into the Al Anbar Province when 40 to 60 insurgents in well-fortified and concealed positions initiated an ambush. Witnessing a rocket-propelled grenade crippling his lead vehicle and while mortar and machine gun fire erupted, he ordered his remaining two vehicles to secure a flanking position. Captain Morel left his vehicle and led a determined assault across an open field and up a 10-foot berm, in order to maneuver into firing positions. The boldness of this first assault eliminated several insurgents at close range, forcing their retreat. Observing his marines pinned down from enemy fire, Captain Morel left the safety of his position and continued the assault, eliminating the enemy's attack. During this valiant act, he fell mortally wounded by a withering burst of enemy automatic weapons fire. By his outstanding display of decisive leadership, unlimited courage in the face of heavy enemy fire, and utmost devotion to duty, Captain Morel reflected great credit upon himself and upheld the highest traditions of the Marine Corps and the United States Naval Service.

OFFICIAL NAVY CROSS CITATION

The President of the United States
takes pleasure in presenting
the Navy Cross
to

Willie Copeland III
United States Marine Corps

for service as set forth in the following:

The Navy Cross is awarded to Sergeant Willie L. Copeland III, United States Marine Corps, for extraordinary heroism as Team Leader, 2nd Platoon, Bravo Company, 1st Reconnaissance Battalion, 1st Marine Division, I Marine Expeditionary Force, U.S. Marine Corps Forces, Central Command in support of Operation Iraqi Freedom on April 7, 2004. Tasked as the Main Effort to lead a convoy to a Forward Operating Base, Sergeant Copeland's platoon was ambushed by 40 to 60 insurgents in well-fortified and concealed positions near the province of Al Anbar. After observing a rocket-propelled grenade instantly crippling the lead vehicle and having mortar and machine gun fire disable his own, Sergeant Copeland led five marines out of the heaviest zone under attack and made an assault across an open field. They continued the assault across a deep and muddy canal, working their way up to firing positions on the far side within hand grenade range of the enemy. The vigor of this first assault eliminated ten insurgents at close range while forcing other enemy positions to flee. During this valiant effort, his commanding officer fell wounded at his side. Unwilling to subject any more marines to danger, he signaled others to remain in covered positions. While placing himself in a position to shield his wounded officer, he applied first aid. Without regard for his own personal safety, Sergeant Copeland stabilized, then evacuated his captain to a safe area. He then conducted the withdrawal of his team from their covered positions through the use of hand grenades. By his bold leadership, wise judgment, and complete dedication to duty, Sergeant Copeland reflected great credit upon himself and upheld the highest traditions of the Marine Corps and the United States Naval Service.

12

Army Lieutenant Colonel Mark Mitchell
DISTINGUISHED SERVICE CROSS

AFGHANISTAN

The cause of liberty is being advanced day in and day out by American soldiers, sailors, airmen, and marines on the ground. History will vindicate our efforts. I have no doubt in my mind.

—LIEUTENANT COLONEL MARK MITCHELL

Looking out over the audience gathered to witness him receive the first Distinguished Service Cross awarded since the Vietnam War, then-Major Mark Mitchell stopped his eyes on the face of the woman whose husband he had risked everything to posthumously repatriate. Shannon Spann was now a widow, and her husband, CIA Intelligence Officer Johnny "Mike" Spann, had taken his place in history as the first U.S. combat death in the War on Terror. Seated just a few rows from the front, Mrs. Spann had come to pay tribute to Major Mitchell. As their eyes met, a wave of emotion rolled over the soon to be highly decorated Special Forces officer.

"To Mrs. Shannon Spann," he said, still looking at her, "for your personal sacrifice, which is an inspiration to us all, I'm honored to have served with your husband and to have you share this day with me and my family."

Stepping down from the stage, Mitchell then presented a bouquet of flowers to Shannon Spann before hugging her.

The emotion-filled moment marked the culmination of what had been the most harrowing experience of Mitchell's distinguished career. To be sure, *every* battle in war can prove pivotal. But had Major Mitchell not led his fifteen-man Special Forces team against the five hundred to six hundred al Qaeda and Taliban fighters who had taken over the gigantic Qala-i-Jangi Fortress in Mazar-e-Sharif, Afghanistan, the highly successful first phase of the War on Terrorism might have turned out differently, much differently. "It would have been very, very, serious," said Navy Commander Kevin Aandahl, a spokesman at U.S. Central Command.[1]

Even so, most Americans don't know the story behind the heroic battle Mitchell and his men waged. In some ways, knowledge of these events had fallen victim to Mitchell's success, as media organizations swarmed to report on one of the prisoners captured as the result of his actions, the so-called American Taliban, John Walker Lindh. But the oversight and lack of national attention to himself hardly bothered the exceedingly humble Mitchell. After all, Green Berets are frequently called "the quiet professionals." Nevertheless there is a reason Lieutenant Colonel Mitchell was the first soldier since Vietnam to receive the Distinguished Service Cross. And his David-versus-Goliath–like story, while overshadowed by the mainstream media's fixation with the American Taliban, is worthy of national remembrance.

That Lieutenant Colonel Mark Mitchell was destined to become a leader is hardly surprising. Going back to his youth, one finds the signs of great things to come. While attending high school in Milwaukee, Wisconsin, Mitchell had proven unusually driven for a young man his age. Each morning, while his fellow classmates filed in zombielike fashion into his all-boy Jesuit high school, Mitchell had already been awake and working for several hours. By four thirty A.M. he was out the door and delivering newspapers. After school, it was off to wrestling practice before heading to his second job at the local Irish pub where he stocked the bar and vacuumed floors. His highly disciplined, sleep-deprived schedule proved prescient.

In August 1983, Mitchell received an ROTC scholarship to attend Marquette University, where he majored in biomedical engineering. Following graduation, he was commissioned in the infantry and, after training at Fort Benning, Georgia, reported to his first assignment at Fort Stewart, Georgia. After returning from fighting in the first Gulf War, Mitchell was approached about entering the assessment and selection process for the army's Special Forces.

The challenging and competitive nature of it all appealed to his ultradisciplined and driven nature. "You are given a sense of responsibility and autonomy that you do not get in any other unit," said Mitchell. "The soldiers here are the ultimate professional soldiers. They have so many talents. The dropout rate is close to seventy percent."

Special Forces (SF) soldiers go through some of the most grueling training in the U.S. military. The three-week assessment and selection process stretches men to their intellectual, emotional, and physical limits. In addition to physical stamina and strength, potential recruits are expected to employ strong interpersonal communication skills, cross-cultural communication skills, analytical reasoning skills, and a high degree of prudent judgment. These traits are all evaluated during the infamous "Robin Sage" exercise. This two-week-long fictional warfare scenario drops would-be Green Berets in the middle of the woods deep behind enemy lines. The events that unfold are based on actual military encounters and are loosely scripted in order to allow officers to exploit any potential weaknesses perceived in the individual being evaluated. Civilian volunteers are also used to make the experience more realistic. Adaptability, physicality, negotiation, and the ability to persuade are all held at a high premium, but potential recruits are given no evaluation criteria.

"They never tell you what the standard is; they just tell you to do your best. The training is extremely mentally demanding. When I was in Afghanistan there were several times when I looked back on my Robin Sage and thought, 'This situation is almost identical to the one I was put in during my assessment and selection.'"

However, despite the stellar training Special Forces receive, it is hard to envision that *any* exercise could have readied Mitchell for the experience he would encounter over four days at the Qala-i-Jangi fortress near Mazar-e-Sharif, Afghanistan, in 2001.

The date was November 25, 2001. It had been twenty-three days since a rotary-wing aircraft had dropped Mitchell and eight other Special Forces soldiers into Afghanistan at three A.M. Mitchell and his men had spent the intervening three weeks engaged in rapid movement and fighting. For a time, he had taken up residence in the Qala-i-Jangi fortress, which literally—if ominously—translates as "House of War." Built in the nineteenth century, the structure measures roughly a half mile across in each direction and is surrounded by thirty-five-foot walls made of mud and straw brick. Qala-i-Jangi is divided in half by an interior wall, which, in aerial photos at least, resembles the center line of a basketball court. In its center was an entryway known simply as the "fatal funnel." This opening was flanked on the wall's southern side by two enormous armories, which had been stocked with numerous armaments, including RPG launchers, AK-47s, and mortars.

There were other buildings inside the fortress as well, such as the "pink schoolhouse," a reinforced concrete building with a bunkerlike basement. Initially, Mitchell and others used a large two-story building at the north end of the fortress as a makeshift residence. It also doubled as a headquarters for Northern Alliance leader General Abdul Rashid Dostum. The accommodations were humble, to say the least. There was no running water, and a small generator supplied all of the electricity. Furthermore, Mitchell says that, in order to prevent poisoning, he and the others had to hire trustworthy Afghans to purchase their daily rations of pita bread and local foods from different markets.

By late November, however, coalition forces appeared to be on a roll in northern Afghanistan. Mazar-e-Sharif had been liberated two weeks earlier, Taliban and al Qaeda forces were on the run, and the siege at Konduz was shaping up to be what many believed would be the final, climactic battle in northern Afghanistan. Intelligence reports indicated that over eight thousand Taliban and al Qaeda fighters had gathered in Konduz and were preparing to defend the city. General Abdul Rashid Dostum and other leaders of the Northern Alliance marshaled their forces in Mazar-e-Sharif and headed east to Konduz. As they departed Mazar-e-Sharif, they encountered a convoy of five hundred to six hundred enemy fighters that included many al Qaeda–trained foreign fighters. After several hours of intense negotiations and a suicide attack that killed General Dostum's intelligence chief, the U.S. ally ordered his men to search and detain the surrendered enemy fighters at the Qala-i-Jangi fortress. The enemy prisoners were transported to Qala-i-Jangi in the same trucks they had driven from Konduz. General Dostum and the overwhelming majority of Northern Alliance forces and their American advisors continued on to Konduz, leaving only about one hundred Northern Alliance soldiers to guard the prisoners that night. Later that evening, a second suicide bomber detonated himself inside the fortress, killing several Northern Alliance soldiers.

The following morning, two Americans, both CIA agents, went to Qala-i-Jangi to interrogate selected prisoners. They were among only a handful of Americans remaining in Mazar-e-Sharif. It was the job of these two men—Johnny "Mike" Spann and another agent identified publicly only as "Dave"—to question the terrorist prisoners on the whereabouts of Osama bin Laden.

General Dostum's departure and the generally poor living conditions at Qala-i-Jangi had forced Mitchell and the others to relocate their headquarters to the "Turkish School," a high school fifteen miles away. This building, a gift from the people of Turkey to the city of Mazar-e-Sharif, was surrounded by a gate and, at only five stories tall, was the tallest structure in town.

Around noon local time, Major Mitchell received word that one of General Dostum's lieutenants was at the front gate and needed to speak with him immediately.

"There's been an uprising at the fortress!" the man said frantically. "We need you and your men there at once!"

The Taliban and al Qaeda prisoners had not been properly searched and had smuggled numerous weapons into the fortress. Many military analysts now believe the surrender east of Mazar-e-Sharif may have actually been part of a "Trojan horse" tactic designed to draw closer to coalition forces in the hopes of recapturing Mazar-e-Sharif. Whatever their motivation, the enemy fighters had successfully exploited two cultural mind-sets operative in General Dostum and his men. First, having captured fellow Muslims, the Northern Alliance soldiers had been naturally respectful and trusting of the prisoners' common heritage and beliefs. And second, among Afghans there is a belief that a man's word is his bond: If he says he surrenders, he surrenders. What the Northern Alliance fighters had failed to take into account, however, was that many of those captured weren't Afghans and were instead a younger breed who believed that lying to "the Infidels" was permissible if it furthered their jihad.

But none of this mattered now. Mitchell knew the situation was dire. Worse, by the time the uprising began, most of the Americans had already gone to assist with the surrender at Konduz. Major Mitchell and Battalion Executive Officer Major

Kurt Sonntag had only a handful of Special Forces soldiers on the ground in Mazar-e-Sharif.

"We didn't have a lot of time," recalls Mitchell. "So I gathered a 'pickup team' consisting of seven British SAS [Special Air Service—the British equivalent of U.S. Special Forces], one U.S. Navy SEAL, and six army Special Forces soldiers. The British contingent had literally arrived the night before and were still adjusting to their surroundings but were eager to join in the mission."

The fifteen elite soldiers hustled to gather their gear while Mitchell outlined the strategic and tactical considerations. Within thirty minutes they were packed and racing down the stairs before jamming into four SUVs. Three of the vehicles, Range Rovers, belonged to the Britons. Each had a 762 general-purpose machine gun (GPMG) similar to the U.S. M-240 mounted on top. Due to British restrictions, the vehicles were painted white. "They stuck out like a sore thumb," Mitchell recalls.

The fourth vehicle, U.S. owned, wasn't much better. It was a green, civilian Toyota 4Runner that Mitchell and his men had purchased from some locals in town.

"I drove the lead vehicle. It was my first time driving a right-hand-drive manual transmission. The steering column and suspension on this thing *really* needed some work. I remember feeling it sway when we went around corners."

With his SUV's tires crunching the gravel beneath them, Mitchell hoped the jostling vehicle wouldn't quit out on them. But he had bigger worries on his mind. He was concerned the enemy fighters might have gotten loose and would engage them as they wound through the bustling market square. At one point, a truck pulled out in front of Mitchell's vehicle and slammed on the brakes. Mitchell yanked the steering wheel and zipped around the potential terrorist-filled truck.

"Nice job!" said one of the Special Forces soldiers.

Now on the far side of Mazar-e-Sharif, Mitchell floored his 4Runner to sixty mph, a high speed considering the rough-hewn roads and the SUV's shoddy suspension. When they finally arrived, Mitchell stopped at a small village about one hundred meters from the main fortress gate to assess the situation. Having lived inside Qala-i-Jangi, Major Mitchell was well acquainted with the interior layout. Still, sneaking into the terrorist-infested structure would need to be done stealthily. The elite SF team could see their Northern Alliance allies inside the main gate, a good sign the Taliban and al Qaeda prisoners had not yet overpowered General Dostum's men.

With the crack of small-arms fire filling the air, Mitchell's team would have to expose themselves while crossing the open area leading to the main fortress gate. Mitchell decided to take two of the British trucks with mounted machine guns as cover while he and his fellow Green Berets ran alongside the vehicles. The stark white Range Rovers rolled in through the front gates without incident. Mitchell and his men were now inside the "House of War."

Mitchell quickly realized that if the prisoners were able to seize the fortress with its huge stockpile of weapons, the capture of Mazar-e-Sharif could be in jeopardy. Admittedly, having only one hundred Northern Alliance soldiers and two CIA agents available to help fend off five hundred terrorists was less than ideal. But Special Forces adhere to a common dictum: "Remain flexible. Everything may go wrong, so deal with it."

Major Mitchell looked around for a familiar face. That's when he found Fakir, one of General Dostum's lieutenants. Fakir didn't speak any English, but Mitchell was able to ask where "Baba Daoud" (Dave) was. Fakir whipped out his radio and somehow managed to pick Dave up.

"Dave told me what had happened," said Mitchell. "I asked him where Mike [Spann] was. He was pretty adamant that he thought Mike was dead. He had last seen his body motionless in the opening minutes of the battle. From his voice over the radio I could tell he was very upset and that he was in a bad position. So I told him, 'We're going to come get you.' But I also said, 'If you get an opportunity, get on the roof and go over the back wall.'"

Mitchell quickly scanned the interior of the fortress he had once called home. He and his men had entered on the northern side, which the Northern Alliance still controlled. But the southern side—the side over the center wall—which had access to the armories, was now under the control of the Taliban and al Qaeda prisoners.

None of the Special Forces soldiers wore body armor or helmets; their Afghan counterparts didn't have them, so they had not even packed them when preparing to infiltrate Afghanistan. Besides, doing so would have only drawn unwanted attention. As for weapons, Mitchell carried an M-4 Carbine and his 9mm pistol. After directing the British SAS to set up their machine guns to prevent enemy movement toward the main gate, Mitchell signaled his SF team to move around the exterior wall, closer to Dave's reported location. It was the only thing separating them from the five hundred Taliban and al Qaeda terrorists. As they ran, a mortar jolted the ground fifty feet directly behind them. When they got to the wall, Mitchell and the others began clawing their way up the steep thirty-foot structure.

With their bare hands, the soldiers crawled like spiders up the towering edifice. Enemy bullets sailed over the top of the wall as they climbed. The structure's angle seemed to grow impossibly steep, but they still hadn't reached the top.

"Fakir yelled up at the wall," remembers Mitchell. "One of the Northern Alliance soldiers poked his head over. He looked surprised to see us. We motioned for him to reach over and give us a hand, but it was too far for him to reach; we still had about six feet to go. So he reached up and pulled his turban off his head and unraveled it. It was blue-and-green plaid, the type commonly worn by the Hazarahs, descendants of the Mongols who had invaded Afghanistan in the thirteenth century. He wrapped one end around one of his hands. We grabbed hold of the unraveled turban and pulled ourselves up to the top of the wall."

As soon as the SF soldiers climbed atop the wall, RPGs zipped through the air. "Get down!" the leader yelled.

Mitchell's men dropped to the dirt and ducked behind the tiny two-and-a-half–foot ledge that lined the edge of the wall. Mitchell then looked out over the southern side of the wall. The number of Taliban and al Qaeda prisoners was dizzying. He also looked for Dave, but he was nowhere to be found.

The calculus of the situation had to change and fast. The enemy was knocking out Northern Alliance soldiers left and right. With each passing minute, the terrorists pulled more and more weapons from the huge fortress armories. That's when Mitchell turned to his Air Force combat controller. It was about four P.M.

The wall they were sitting on was 150 meters—just one and a half football fields—away from the terrorist nests. Mitchell wanted to pulverize them with 2,000-pound JDAM bombs. Although guided by GPS, the drops would have to be exact. Mitchell understood that what he was about to do was enormously dangerous, but the mission demanded that it be done.

Mitchell looked at his combat controller and gave the signal. "Thirty seconds!" the combat controller yelled into the radio. That was the signal that the Navy F-18s had made the drop and also represented the time remaining until the bombs would come streaking across the sky to unleash their lethal payload. Everybody pressed themselves into the dirt, plugged their ears, and opened their mouths to reduce the impact of the overpressure created by the enormous blast.

"We were having to call these bombs in almost on top of our position, much closer than you'd really like to," said Mitchell.

The first bomb cratered the ground moving 300 mph.

"This enormous mushroom cloud from the explosion instantly shot up hundreds of feet into the air. All I could see was dust," said Mitchell.

The Special Forces soldiers proceeded to call in JDAM after JDAM, a total of eight. Around five thirty P.M. Mitchell and another intelligence officer ran under cover of one of the bombs, scaled another fortress wall under fire, and searched for Dave in the heavily damaged two-story building that had been their home only days earlier. But by then Dave was gone. The JDAMs had given him the cover he needed to sneak over the fortress walls. Because Dave was a language specialist and was fluent in the local language, he had hailed a taxicab and fled the area.

Major Mitchell and the fourteen other Special Forces soldiers returned to their headquarters across town and regrouped. Mitchell says he didn't sleep that night. Instead, he stayed up and planned the second day's actions. He decided that he and his team would go back to Qala-i-Jangi just before first light.

Between planning and preparations the soldiers pulled sentry duty to guard against enemy assaults on their compound. The prisoner convoy had inexplicably stopped right in front of their location the previous day and had seen American soldiers in the compound.

When they arrived on the scene the second day, they were surprised by what they saw: "By now, a gaggle of reporters had gathered outside the fortress, and to my amazement, there was still fighting going on inside between the Northern Alliance and the Taliban and al Qaeda. They had killed a lot of the Northern Alliance guys, were well trained, and knew what they were doing. But I was amazed that after dropping eight JDAMS, 2,000-pound bombs, they were still willing to fight. And that said to me, 'These guys are going to fight to the death.'"

Mitchell and his men snuck back into the fortress. This time they split up into two groups, positioning themselves on opposite sides of the fortress. But when Mitchell's combat controller called in the first air strike, this time something went wrong. Horribly wrong.

"As the first one came in it went astray. The dust starts to clear and I can see some of my guys on the other side of the fortress. The word I was receiving is that they were severely wounded. It was nine guys: four Brits, four SF guys, and one Air Force combat controller. There were some walking wounded, but others were disoriented and bleeding from their nose and ears. They're covered head-to-toe in brown dust. I mean they're *caked* in it."

Mitchell immediately called off any air strikes. He had to get his guys out of the fortress and medevac them to safety. Doing so wouldn't be easy: Because their actions were covert, there were no aircraft stationed in Mazar-e-Sharif. What's more, the U.S. Air Force had successfully cratered the only airstrip, leaving helicopters as the only means to evacuate the wounded. That meant the only thing they could do was to wait for helicopters to fly all the way from Uzbekistan. So they waited for three hours, the time it took the helicopters to arrive before Mitchell could evacuate the wounded from the fortress. Luckily, the battalion surgeon and several highly trained SF medics were among those not wounded and were able to provide the injured soldiers with life-saving treatment.

Having just lost over half his team and having spent almost the entire day evacuating the wounded, Mitchell stood outside the Turkish School and thought about his comrades and the ancient fortress still festering with terrorists. Nine of his men had been sidelined, leaving only five others and himself.

"By this point I'm determined," Mitchell told us. "Frankly, I'm pissed off and determined to see this thing through to victory. So we made plans that night to go back in under the cover of darkness. It was the first night an AC-130 Spectre gunship was available. At about nine P.M., me and the five others went back in with about ten Afghans. The first gunship didn't show up because it had mechanical problems and was forced to return to base. So we were in the fortress alone and waiting for about two hours.

"There was a lot of mortar fire being directed at our position. These guys were really sophisticated. In fact, we later found the U.S. charge tables that they had been using. They must have been able to read them, estimate the range to our position, and put the correct charge on there. The mortars were coming in all around us. So the first AC-130 expends all its ammo. The second aircraft was down to their last six rounds of 105mm ammo and had expended all their other ammo. I then heard, 'Got it! Got it!' They hit the building with the mortar guys. The building was loaded to the gills with rockets and RPGs and everything. It was like a small mushroom cloud in the dark of the night, and then you see this 150-to 200-foot ball of flame. We were getting showered by debris, the weapons were cooking off, and you could feel the shockwave and the heat. It was pretty intense."

The floor of the massive fortress was now littered with the shredded bodies of Taliban and al Qaeda terrorists. Against all odds, Major Mitchell had led his five remaining SF soldiers into the fortress to guide U.S. fighter pilots to their terrorist targets and away from America's Northern Alliance allies. As former CIA Director George Tenet later put it, "In a world where most flee from danger, Major Mark Mitchell belongs to that few who go forward."[2]

But Mitchell wasn't satisfied. The uprising had not been quelled completely. Moreover, CIA Agent Johnny "Mike" Spann's body had yet to be recovered.

That night, back at Mitchell's headquarters, located fifteen miles across town, the blazing ball of fire in the fortress was still visible. Mitchell slept only two hours. By day three, the Northern Alliance forces had begun trickling back in from Konduz. Tanks and reinforcements from the Tenth Mountain Division were also beginning to arrive at the fortress. Unbelievably, the remaining terrorists still fought on. Regardless, Mitchell was determined to see to it that Agent Spann's body was located and recovered. And it was.

"We did not want all the reporters coming up snapping pictures of the body, à la Mogadishu," said Mitchell. "So out of respect for Mike, we were very conscious that we not let that happen."

Major Mitchell helped carry Agent Spann's body outside the fortress. U.S. officials later concluded that Agent Johnny Spann had been shot in the head in the early stages of the prisoner uprising.

"We all carried the body bag onto the helicopter. It was a pretty emotional event putting him on that aircraft," Mitchell confessed.

Even after the recovery of Agent Spann's body, Taliban and al Qaeda fighters continued battling inside the fortress. The remaining one hundred enemy fighters had hunkered down inside the pink schoolhouse basement, the same structure

Mitchell had once called home. General Dostum was now back from Konduz. When he had a mullah coax them to come out, the terrorists still refused. It wasn't until the Northern Alliance soldiers flooded the basement with water that the stalwart fighters crawled out of their hole.

Among those who emerged from the basement was U.S. citizen John Walker Lindh, the twenty-year-old Islamic convert from upscale Marin County, California, a place *Newsweek* calls "possibly the most liberal, tolerant place in America."[3] The rich kid-turned-terrorist had been named for one of his parents' heroes, Beatles lead singer John Lennon. Lindh was also one of the last people to come in contact with CIA Agent Johnny "Mike" Spann before he was killed. As their videotaped interrogation session later revealed, Spann had tried to get Lindh to speak:

"All I want to do is talk to you and find out what your story is," Spann told Lindh. "I know you speak English. . . . Do you know the people here you're working with are terrorists and killed other Muslims? There were several hundred Muslims killed in the bombing in New York City. Is that what the Quran teaches? I don't think so."[4]

Yet for all Spann's attempts to begin a dialogue, Lindh sat in stoic defiance. Shortly after their exchange, Spann was shot in the head by Lindh's fellow jihadists.

Several months after the battle at Qala-i-Jangi fortress, Mark Mitchell finally returned to the United States. Prior to his February departure, Mitchell spearheaded numerous efforts, including the seemingly impossible task of helping repair the crater-riddled Mazar-e-Sharif runway using little more than pickup trucks full of smooth river rock and tar, a feat that allowed over two hundred aircraft to land safely. But it was Mitchell's dogged determination to defeat the terrorist uprising in the "House of War" that resulted in his receiving the Distinguished Service Cross. In the end, Mitchell's leadership had led to the elimination of over four hundred terrorists.

It had been months since he had spoken to his wife. His youngest child was only one and a half years old the day he left for Afghanistan. The last thing he had done was write a final letter to his wife and children in the event he didn't make it back home alive. "Writing that letter was one of the hardest things I've ever had to do," Mitchell said.

Also difficult for him has been listening to the barrage of criticism the media have aimed at the soldiers, sailors, airmen, and marines waging the War on Terror. "I get very frustrated, very agitated, to hear the criticisms that are leveled. I tell my family, my friends, and anyone who will listen that the truth is that Afghanistan and Iraq are today far better off than they would be had we not taken any action. War is a messy business, and there are going to be setbacks. But soldiers, sailors, airmen, and marines—we have a way of insulating ourselves from the politics and not taking that stuff [attacks by critics] to heart. We have a mission to focus on. We all signed up to serve our country, and we're not going to let the naysayers dissuade us from doing so."

For Lieutenant Colonel Mitchell, remaining focused on the mission means remembering the event that prompted America's entry into the War on Terror: "I will never forget September 11. That's what started this. That's why we're out here. I hear a lot of young soldiers say, 'That's why I signed up.' . . .

We are winning the war on terrorism in the big picture. We're not the ones who were summarily executing women and children in Afghanistan. We're not the ones who filled the mass graves in Iraq. We're not the ones that are blowing up people in the market and using airliners or WMD against their own people. The cause of liberty is being advanced day in and day out by American soldiers, sailors, airmen, and marines on the ground. History will vindicate our efforts. I have no doubt in my mind."

While Lieutenant Colonel Mitchell remains steadfast on the merits of America's mission, he is less certain as to whether his actions warranted the Distinguished Service Cross: "I'm still not convinced I deserved this. All I expected was a pat on the back and a job well done. I'm still the same guy. My outlook on life, my beliefs, the things that are important to me are all the same. I thank God that I've had an opportunity to serve my country. And that I've had the opportunity to come home again and see my kids and wife."

Standing on stage preparing to receive the first Distinguished Service Cross awarded in over a quarter century, it was this last blessing—the ability to return home to his wife and children—that flooded his mind the second his eyes found Shannon Spann's in the audience. It was a difficult moment but an important one, a moment Mitchell says reminds him of the cause for which Johnny Spann died.

"I think too many Americans have forgotten what started this on September 11. If we forget, we will lose our vigilance."

OFFICIAL DISTINGUISHED SERVICE
CROSS CITATION

The President of the United States
takes pleasure in presenting
the Distinguished Service Cross

to

Mark Mitchell
United States Army

for service as set forth in the following:

For extraordinary heroism while serving with Headquarters and Headquarters Detachment, 3d Battalion, 5th Special Forces Group (Airborne), during the period of 25 to 28 November 2001, Major Mitchell distinguished himself while engaged in combat operations during Operation Enduring Freedom. As the Ground Force Commander of a rescue operation during the Battle of Qala-i-Jangi Fortress, Mazar-e-Sharif, Afghanistan, Major Mitchell ensured the freedom of one American and the posthumous repatriation of another. His unparalleled courage under fire, decisive leadership and personal sacrifice were directly responsible for the success of the rescue operation and were further instrumental in ensuring the city of Mazar-e-Sharif did not fall back in the hands of the Taliban. His personal example has added yet another laurel to the proud military history of this Nation and serves as the standard for all others to emulate. Major Mitchell's gallant deed was truly above and beyond the call of duty and is in keeping with the finest traditions of the military service and reflects great credit upon himself, the 5th Special Forces Group (Airborne), the United States Army, and the United States of America.

13

Army Sergeant First Class Paul Ray Smith
MEDAL OF HONOR

IRAQ

> Scripture tells us . . . that a man has no greater love than to lay down his life for his friends. And that is exactly the responsibility Paul Smith believed the sergeant stripes on his sleeve had given him.
>
> **—PRESIDENT GEORGE W. BUSH**

The day had finally arrived. Sergeant First Class Paul Ray Smith, a member of the legendary "Rock of the Marne," the Third Infantry Division, was heading to Iraq. As with all soldiers, the day had been a mixture of anxiety, sadness, and anticipation. Just before making his final departure, Smith, thirty-three, said good-bye to his wife, Birgit, and his stepdaughter, Jessica, before looking down at his young son, David. He searched for the right words to say.

"You're the man in the house now," he said.[1]

But what Sergeant First Class Smith didn't say—indeed, what he *couldn't* have said—was that young David would soon bear another title: the son of the only American soldier in the War on Terror to have been awarded the Medal of Honor.

It is impossible to overstate the Medal of Honor's importance and significance. By law, the medal may only be awarded by the president of the United States on behalf of the Congress. The medal recognizes a man or woman in the armed services who, while engaged with an enemy in combat, "distinguished him- or herself conspicuously by gallantry and intrepidity," and thus served "above and beyond the call of duty." This is a phrase many Americans use whether they know its origins or not. But in terms of the Medal of Honor, it means that no matter the level of heroism exhibited in battle, the medal may only be awarded to those individuals whose gallantry and valor were displayed *outside of* a direct order and therefore represented an act of complete selflessness.[2] As if that threshold weren't high enough, any GI recommended for the award must pass a twelve-level review through the military chain of command before reaching the president for his ultimate approval.

For this reason, the award rightly embodies an iconic, larger-than-life quality. In his book, *Medal of Honor*, Allen Mikaelian writes that General George Patton so coveted the award that he said he would have given his "soul" to be awarded one. Likewise, presidents Lyndon Baines Johnson and Harry S Truman said they would rather have been awarded the Medal of Honor than to have been president of the United States.[3]

The numbers explain why. Since the Civil War, only 3,439 men and 1 woman have been awarded the Medal of Honor. Only 129 men alive today have one. And while Sergeant First

Class Smith belongs to the former group, tragically, he does not belong to the latter. Indeed, without the unbelievable bravery and heroism Smith displayed on April 4, 2003, several of his men would undoubtedly have never lived to tell his story.

Paul Smith grew up not far from the long, winding, white-columned sidewalk that lines Bayshore Boulevard in south Tampa. Like the currents that gather in the bay for which his hometown is named, Smith's early life experiences seemed random, aimless, choppy. Paul always loved discovering things, like shells and rocks, while wading through the ocean. The salty waters, Smith understood, merely masked the treasures deep within.

Smith soon learned that Palma Ceia, the area in south Tampa where he grew up, could be a difficult place to fit in, especially for an El Paso, Texas, transplant like himself. Born on September 24, 1969, his family had moved when he was nine years old. And even though he enjoyed football—the Tampa Bay Buccaneers was his favorite team—his lanky frame and mediocre athletic talents forced him to search for other ways to get involved.

Attending Tampa Bay Technical High School gave him the chance to do things with his hands, such as carpentry and auto mechanics. Yet despite these varied interests, as his U.S. Army biography notes, Paul's family says that for as long as they can remember, the young man's future plans always remained the same: "I want to be a soldier, get married, and have kids." To some, his plan sounded uneventful, uninspiring, boring even. But it was his life; it was his dream.

In 1988, Smith graduated from high school and set in motion the first phase of that dream when he began basic training at Fort Leonard Wood, Missouri. He was trained as a combat engineer and was soon shipped off to Bamberg, Germany. Back then, Paul Smith did not appear to possess the attributes of a potential Medal of Honor recipient. Indeed, as President George W. Bush joked during his dedication ceremony, Smith's penchant for drinking and late nights on the town "occasionally earned him what the army calls 'extra duty.' Scrubbing floors."

It was on one of these outings in June 1990, that Paul Smith met Birgit Bacher, a twenty-three-year-old native of Bayreuth, Germany. Like one domino tumbling into the next, Paul's deployment to Germany soon triggered the second part of his dream: marriage. "In the beginning, he was not my type at all. When we first got together, he was not what I was looking for," remembers Birgit. But that evening, sitting at the Green Goose Bar, a sunglass-wearing soldier with his jean-jacket collar flipped up chatted with the young German woman over the sounds of Bon Jovi.[4] Leaving the bar, Paul and two of his pals walked Birgit and her friend back to the hotel they decided to stay in that evening.

As the women settled into their room, they heard a commotion coming from the street outside their window. There, kneeling on one knee, Birgit looked out the window as her future husband and his two pals reenacted the scene from *Top Gun* in which Tom Cruise and his buddy "Goose" serenade a woman with the soulful sounds of "You've lost that loving feeling."[5]

"Six months later, he was deployed to Saudi Arabia for the

Gulf War. When he came back in April, he was totally changed. It was like I saw a young, funny guy go off to war and back came a very strict man; so grown up so fast. He was a very tough soldier," said Mrs. Smith.[6]

The two got married. Jessica, Birgit's daughter from a previous relationship, came to consider Paul her father. Later, the married couple would have a son of their own, David. But the experience of the first Gulf War had steeled the soldier permanently—his playfulness had turned to precision—and this showed in everything he did, including the way he disciplined the children. When David or Jessica would disobey or fail to carry out his orders, he would make them drop and give him twenty push-ups. "I don't hear you counting," he would bark.[7]

The transformation from aimless army guy to serious soldier had been the result of many factors, not the least of which involved the experience of having an army brother die in his arms, a moment that made his decision to join the army take on new meaning. He loved being a *sapper,* the term for combat engineers who detect and disarm land mines. He had once viewed his combat engineer training as largely theoretical. Now, however, those skills had snapped into focus and had proven vital, real, and serious. Indeed, seriousness and an unyielding pursuit for perfection are common themes one hears in the comments of the men Smith led throughout his military career.

Those who served alongside him in Kosovo, men like now-Captain William T. Pohlmann, recall that Smith's determination, seriousness, and perfectionism were in place long before the courtyard battle that would lead to his receiving the

Medal of Honor. As the platoon leader (PL) for the Assault &
Obstacle (A&O) Platoon of B Company, Eleventh Engineers,
Staff Sergeant Smith (at that time he was a staff sergeant) was
now-Captain William T. Pohlmann's leader, his platoon sergeant. Smith was the man responsible for the overall training
and daily operation of the platoon, while Pohlmann, who was
eight years younger than Smith, was the platoon's planner.
The two men conducted a complete train-up for their deployment to Kosovo, KFOR 3A.

Pohlmann shared his recollections with us:

> Throughout this training Sergeant Smith was very hard on the
> soldiers. He demanded that we do everything better than the
> other two platoons in the company. We trained harder and
> worked longer hours than the others. We were the smallest
> platoon, comprised of vehicle operators. Yet our mission in
> Kosovo was the same as that of the other two sapper platoons
> in the company. We had eight-hour shifts, seven days a week
> for the first two months. Sergeant Smith was absolutely deter-
> mined not to have any accidents or incidents while we were
> there. Before every mission, we conducted thorough pre-
> combat inspections (PCIs) to ensure that our soldiers had
> everything that we needed for the mission. When we came
> back into the camp, we would conduct AARs on the mission
> and trained on everything that Sergeant Smith saw that we
> needed to improve. Every day or night that we were out in
> town, Sergeant Smith would lead a patrol himself. He was
> always out with the soldiers, making sure that they were
> remaining vigilant and aware of the situation around them.

Sergeant Smith would also take time to plan and conduct training for the soldiers above and beyond what any other platoon was doing. He taught the soldiers quick-reaction drills to ensure that they knew how to react when faced with a hostile situation. . . . I understood the methods that Sergeant Smith used and knew that he always had the best in mind. I envied his absolute dedication to the profession of arms as well as his sense of duty and selfless service. He was the embodiment of the seven army values. Most of the soldiers did not like him as a person, some did not like him as a leader, but fortunately we never had to test our training while we were in Kosovo. The mission for us was a success. But if we had, I know that the soldiers would have understood what Sergeant Smith had been trying to teach them. We were, without a doubt, the best platoon in the company, and we owed all of that to Sergeant Smith. . . . In April 2003, when I learned about Sergeant First Class Smith's actions at the courtyard, I was deeply saddened for the loss of such a fine soldier.

However, in no way did his actions surprise me. He was a soldier through and through, and he acted as one of the finest soldiers to serve in this army. It was a true privilege to have known Sergeant First Class Paul Smith. I was one of the lucky few who have had the honor to have served with him.

Smith was the walking embodiment of army rigor and discipline. His men recall that his uniform was always perfectly pressed, his shoes shimmered like mirrors, and that his gear was always in top working order, clean and tight.

CSM Gary Coker, Eleventh Engineer Battalion, described

Sergeant First Class Smith as "Hardcore. Disciplined. Passionate about his soldiers. Amongst his peers—noncommissioned officers—there was no fooling around. They knew this guy was serious business and a pro."[8]

First Sergeant Timothy Campbell, Bravo Company, Eleventh Engineer Battalion, remembers how Smith would respond when his fellow "bulldogs" had not paid attention to detail: "You'd go to the motor pool, and you were to look at vehicles that day and they were packed to go to the field. And if they were not all right, he was offended by that. And that's a good quality to have. He took things personal when they weren't as they should be."[9]

Smith's obsession with detail and perfection engendered frustration among many and anger among a few. They believed he should lighten up, relax. *After all,* they thought, *we're not really going to use this stuff.*

Yet underneath his rough-hewn exterior was a man capable of compassion. Despite his attempts to conceal them, flashes of his true feelings for his men could be seen in his quiet acts of goodness.

Birgit recalls two occasions when her husband's love for his soldiers compelled him to act. "Around Christmastime, one of the soldiers had no money. They had two kids, or even three kids, I think. Paul went out and bought presents and brought food over to help the family out. And they will never forget that.

"Then another time a soldier's little girl was very ill, which had to go forty miles away where we lived. Every night after work, Paul drove up to the hospital to visit—every night—to visit the little girl. He brought her a big teddy bear."[10] The little girl, Elizabeth DeLauter, is now three years old. Elizabeth still sleeps with that bear, whom her mother nicknamed "Smithy."[11]

There had been many other displays of concern and love for his men. Like, for example, the time overseas when a handful of his boys felt the call to be baptized. Sergeant Smith not only encouraged the men, he also showed up to support them and to take pictures of the sacred occasion. When they wanted to get haircuts for their big day, Smith saved them all money by cutting their hair himself. One of the soldiers who would later fight alongside Sergeant Smith during his final battle, Sergeant Matthew Keller, shared this memory during a ceremony to dedicate and rename a post office in Sergeant Smith's memory. "Over there [Iraq] a haircut was basically a shaved head," he told the laughing crowd. "He always complimented us on how we looked when he was done."[12]

On April 4, 2003, the two sides of Sergeant First Class Paul Smith—the clenched-jaw sergeant and the tender-hearted family man—would meld in the crucible of decisive action and leadership. The day had begun early, as the sun beamed hard in the Iraq sky. Smith, thirty-three, led Second Platoon, Bravo Company, Eleventh Engineer Battalion, Third Infantry Division as they assisted Task Force 2-7 Infantry. The night before, the Eleventh Engineers had crossed the Euphrates River. Sergeant Smith had not gotten much sleep.

"The thing I remember most was the speed and continuity of movement," said Lieutenant Colonel Thomas Smith (no relation), Eleventh Engineer Battalion commander. "We had two primary missions on the march to Baghdad, to secure a crossing on the Euphrates River and to take and hold the Baghdad airport."[13]

With the first mission now complete, the men were on the home stretch, the final jaunt to the finish line: Saddam Hussein International Airport. Eleven miles was all that separated them from reaching Baghdad. Thoughts of family and victory filled their minds.

As they rolled into the area surrounding the airport, small-arms fire could be heard cracking in the distance. At the time, this hardly seemed cause for concern; the sound had become common during their time in-country. It was then decided that the Eleventh Engineer Battalion would man a roadblock just outside the Saddam Hussein International Airport.

With the roadblock in place and everything under control, Smith's platoon leader, Captain Brian Borkowski, received a request for engineer support from infantry who wanted to perform reconnaissance just south of their current position. That's when Captain Borkowski put Sergeant Smith in charge of the platoon before riding off in an armored combat earth-mover (ACE).

Shortly thereafter, Smith received orders that they were to build a holding area for enemy prisoners, a standard task. Smith had spotted what he thought would be the perfect holding area: a walled compound near the highway and airport that had previously been used by Saddam's republican guards. The compound featured three walls that formed an enclosed triangular courtyard area with a gate on the far end or top "tip" of the triangle. Overlooking the courtyard was a watchtower, which would allow the soldiers to monitor the prisoners of war from above.

The small-arms fire still bothered Smith, though. He wanted to get a better look at what lay on the other side of the enclosed courtyard. Sergeant Smith ordered a bulldozer to burst through one of the courtyard walls.

Sergeant Matthew Keller, who was with Sergeant Smith, said, "When we first got out there, we were taking a lot of indirect fire, RPGs blowing up in the tops of trees and stuff. We were also getting some sniper fire, and I actually saw the sniper and knocked him down.

"Once the hole was knocked in the wall, they went in and started working on the area. I was still outside, but they apparently sent a couple of soldiers forward to look out the gate at the compound, and that's when the enemy was spotted."[14]

Through the courtyard gate, the soldiers saw between 15 and 20 enemy fighters in fighting positions, approximately 175 meters away. When Sergeant Smith got up to the gate, the size of the enemy had swelled to five times that. With a company-size enemy (approximately 100 fighters) now on their way, the soldiers realized the fighters were equipped with RPG, grenades, and rifles.

Smith told Staff Sergeant Lincoln D. Hollinsaid, the soldier who would later replace Smith and tragically be killed three days later, to immediately call for a Bradley fighting vehicle. Sixteen soldiers versus a hundred armed Iraqis were unacceptable odds. Sergeant Smith desperately needed to tilt the firepower back in his direction—fast. The Bradley arrived soon after Sergeant Smith's call. Entering through the original hole, the Bradley fighting vehicle pushed through the courtyard to where Sergeant Smith was standing at the gate. The vehicle moved through the gate and out into the open and stood face-to-face against the enemy fighters in the field. Smith and three others ran behind the vehicle. Smith then went to the front of the Bradley, totally exposing himself to incoming enemy fire, and shot an AT-4 shoulder-fired antitank weapon while directing the fires of the small fire team.

Meanwhile, some of the enemy fighters had now made their way inside the tower overlooking the courtyard. Having now captured the "aerial" vantage point, the Iraqis further pinned down the U.S. soldiers. Smith knew the Bradley would not be enough, so he called for reinforcements. An M-113 armored personnel carrier with a towing trailer, driven by Sergeant Kevin Yetter, quickly entered the courtyard. At the M-113s .50-caliber mounted machine gun was twenty-three-year-old Sergeant Louis Berwald. As the M-113 rolled toward the Bradley vehicle, Berwald pointed the .50-caliber to the left and began unloading on the enemy-occupied tower.

As the M-113 moved in behind the Bradley and joined in the fight outside the courtyard walls, enemy mortars quickly neutralized Yetter and Berwald's efforts. One of the mortars sent shrapnel whizzing through the air. Yetter and Berwald's faces and bodies were riddled with the flying metal and were now streaming with blood.

With the M-113 now unmanned, the Bradley vehicle did its best to fend off the frontal assault while being pummeled by RPG and mortar rounds. Now low on ammunition, the driver of the Bradley surprised the soldiers on the ground when he threw the vehicle into reverse, maneuvered around the emptied M-113, and nearly ran over the injured Yetter as it backed all the way out of the courtyard.

In his stellar recounting of the scene, *St. Petersburg Times* writer Alex Leary quotes one soldier's response the moment he saw the Bradley leave the fight: "Everyone was like, 'What the hell?' We felt like we got left out there alone."[15]

Sergeant Smith and his men had begun to gain ground only to have it slip away. Berwald, Yetter, and Hill were all injured; the Bradley had fled the scene; the .50-caliber machine gun atop the M-113 was unmanned; and what little firepower the soldiers could muster was further eroded by the need to evacuate the injured men in the courtyard.

Worse still, with enemy fighters raining RPG and mortar rounds less than a football field away, at least one hundred American soldiers were in the immediate vicinity of the courtyard. Were the Iraqis able to overpower Sergeant Smith's men and overtake their position, the officers in a command center as well as a U.S. medical-aid station would be easy targets for the encroaching Iraqi forces.

And that's when Sergeant First Class Paul Smith made the decision that would save one hundred American lives and cost him his own. He climbed inside the vacated M-113 gunner's turret. "Get me a driver," he yelled.[16]

Private Michael Seaman, twenty-one, hopped in the driver's seat. Smith ordered Seaman to back the vehicle into the courtyard so that he would have a clear shot to both the tower and the open gate. Standing behind the .50-caliber machine gun with his upper torso fully exposed, Smith commanded the young private to keep the big machine gun loaded.

Smith's men looked on in awe at the sight before them. Their platoon leader was now single-handedly fending off the enemy force. Swiveling back and forth between the tower and the gate, Sergeant First Class Smith sprayed the enemy with a lethal hail of firepower. No sooner had Sergeant Smith run through the first box of ammo than Private Seaman had reloaded him with a second and then a third. When Private Seaman finished loading Sergeant Smith's .50-caliber machine gun, Smith yelled for the young man to duck back under his hatch.

Smith's wall of firepower forced the Iraqis in the tower to focus in on him, which in turn allowed GIs outside the courtyard to move into position and begin firing directly on the shooters inside the tower.

Suddenly, Sergeant Smith's .50-caliber machine gun fell silent. Private Seaman looked up from his hatch and found his leader slumped over, with blood streaming down the front of his vest and face. A lone Iraqi bullet, most likely from the tower, had hit Sergeant Smith in the head. Some of his men made a valiant effort to save their leader, but it was to no avail. Despite the ferocity of the fight and overwhelming odds, Sergeant Smith was the only soldier to die during the courtyard battle.[17]

However, the same could not be said of the enemy. Sergeant First Class Smith's fearless act of heroism had resulted in the elimination of at least fifty enemy fighters, half the number that had tried to overwhelm his men. He could have easily retreated through the hole in the compound wall, but doing so would have placed his men and the hundred GIs in the area in mortal danger. And that was something Sergeant First Class Paul Ray Smith would never allow.

The soldiers of B Company, Eleventh Engineer Battalion, 3ID knew Sergeant Smith's story and fate, but his wife, Birgit Smith, did not. "The kids were sleeping, and I was sleeping. And then I heard the doorbell and looked out the peephole. There were two soldiers. One of them was E-7, like Paul's rank, and the other was a chaplain," said Birgit. "And the E-7 told me that he had bad news. And I said, 'What?' And he said, 'Paul is dead.' I said, 'Are you sure? Our name is so common.' He said, 'Ma'am, I wouldn't be here if it weren't one hundred percent,'" Mrs. Smith recalls.[18]

Nothing could undo her pain. But the U.S. military and President Bush's final announcement that Paul would receive the Medal of Honor provided Birgit with some solace.

"I know what Paul did had a meaning; it was not for nothing. He just did what he loved to do . . . I'm so grateful. You cannot even put it in words how happy that makes me that with the Medal of Honor, Paul's going to go into history. His name will never die. That is very, very important to me, that his name lives on forever."[19]

During the ceremony at the White House, President George W. Bush spoke about the bravery and heroism Sergeant First Class Smith displayed that April day in the courtyard. As the medal citation was read aloud, the president stood beside Birgit and the children. A large, shadow box–style frame housed the highest honor the U.S. military can bestow upon a soldier, the Medal of Honor. President Bush placed the box into the hands of the young boy who, on the day of his father's departure to Iraq, had been told he was now the man of the house. As audience applause filled the air, flashes from the White House press corps cameras danced over the young boy. David, ten, just held the big box over his heart and looked down at the medal his father would never wear nor see. The president glanced over at Birgit, who now had tears in her eyes, and for a brief moment the president appeared he too might follow her lead.

Birgit and the children then traveled to Arlington Cemetery for the unveiling of Paul's headstone. Young David displayed the face of manhood, serious and focused. As his mother and sister broke down in tears, David, seated between them, gripped his mother's hand and did his best to console and comfort her. And in that moment, David had obeyed his father's final command. Indeed, he had become an embodiment of his hero father: solid and unwavering on the outside, caring and full of love and compassion on the inside.

OFFICIAL MEDAL OF HONOR CITATION

*The President of the United States of America,
authorized by Act of Congress, March 3, 1863, has
awarded in the name of Congress the Medal of Honor*
to

Paul Ray Smith
United States Army

for service as set forth in the following:

*For conspicuous gallantry and intrepidity at the risk of his life
above and beyond the call of duty:*

Sergeant First Class Paul R. Smith distinguished himself by
acts of gallantry and intrepidity above and beyond the call of
duty in action with an armed enemy near Baghdad International
Airport, Baghdad, Iraq, on 4 April 2003. On that day,
Sergeant First Class Smith was engaged in the construction of
a prisoner of war holding area when his Task Force was violently attacked by a company-sized enemy force. Realizing the
vulnerability of over 100 fellow soldiers, Sergeant First Class
Smith quickly organized a hasty defense consisting of two platoons of soldiers, one Bradley Fighting Vehicle and three armored personnel carriers. As the fight developed, Sergeant
First Class Smith braved hostile enemy fire to personally engage the enemy with hand grenades and anti-tank weapons,
and organized the evacuation of three wounded soldiers from
an armored personnel carrier struck by a rocket propelled
grenade and a 60 mm mortar round. Fearing the enemy would
overrun their defenses, Sergeant First Class Smith moved under

withering enemy fire to man a .50 caliber machine gun mounted on a damaged armored personnel carrier. In total disregard for his own life, he maintained his exposed position in order to engage the attacking enemy force. During this action, he was mortally wounded. His courageous actions helped defeat the enemy attack, and resulted in as many as 50 enemy soldiers killed, while allowing the safe withdrawal of numerous wounded soldiers. Sergeant First Class Smith's extraordinary heroism and uncommon valor are in keeping with the highest traditions of the military service and reflect great credit upon himself, the Third Infantry Division "Rock of the Marne," and the United States Army.

14

Marine Sergeant Rafael Peralta
PURPLE HEART
NOMINATED FOR THE MEDAL OF HONOR

IRAQ

Be proud of being an American. Our father came to this country, became a citizen because it was the right place for our family to be.

**—SERGEANT PERALTA'S FINAL LETTER
TO HIS YOUNGER BROTHER, RICARDO**

Rafael Peralta was not born in America, but he died defending her. "It's the stuff you hear about in boot camp, about World War II and Tarawa marines who won the Medal of Honor," said Corporal Rob Rogers, one of Peralta's platoon mates.[1]

A Mexican immigrant, Peralta joined the marines the day he received his green card. His love for America was no secret; it showed in everything he did. Even the walls of his bedroom were a testament to his patriotism. On them he had hung a picture of his boot camp graduation and replicas of the Declaration of Independence and the Bill of Rights.[2] But ultimately it was Marine Sergeant Peralta's actions on November 15, 2004, while serving as part of Alpha Company, First Battalion,

Third Marine Regiment that proved the depth of his devotion to his country.

Just days prior, Peralta had sat down and written his first and final letters to his brother and youngest sister: "Tomorrow, at 19:00 hours [seven P.M.], we are going to declare war in the holy city of Fallujah. We are going to defeat the insurgents. Watch the news, it's going to be all over. Be proud of me, bro, I'm going to make history and do something that I always wanted to do."[3]

As his story reveals, Marine Sergeant Rafael Peralta kept his word.

It had been almost a year since her tragic death, and yet still, Rafael Peralta's recurring dream about his fiancée, Maritca Alvarez, just wouldn't go away. Maritca and Rafael had met in a Tijuana nightclub two years before their engagement. Even after his family had moved from Mexico to San Diego, his father continued the commute to Tijuana, where he worked as a diesel mechanic. In September 2001, Rafael had been deployed overseas the day his father died. It was Sergeant Peralta's memory of the pride his father had displayed the day he had become an American citizen that had in part inspired him to become a marine. That meant that his mother, Rosa, a housekeeper, would be forced to face her husband's death without her oldest son at her side. Yet it wasn't before long that Sergeant Peralta began to assume his father's mantle as head of the family.[4]

The death of Peralta's father would be just the first in a series of tragic events that would soon unfold. Just days before Rafael and Maritca were to be married, Maritca's mother died. Then, while traveling to bury her, Maritca herself was killed in a truck accident. Having just lost his future mother-in-law and wife in a matter of days, Rafael and his mother bonded in the way that only people who have lost the loves of their life can.[5]

So when Sergeant Peralta shared his recurring dream with his mother, she remembered it. Rafael said he would see Maritca's face. She would approach him. And then Maritca would say that she had come to take him with her so that they could be together again. He knew his actions in battle might one day turn his dream into reality, and he had prepared himself and those he loved should he ever meet his fate on the battlefield. "He said he was ready to die," said his oldest sister, Icela Donald. "He had reconciled with God and [he wanted Rosa] to be strong. She had to take care of my little sister and brother. He would always tell my mom that there was a possibility that he might not come back."[6]

And perhaps it was this sentiment that drove Sergeant Peralta to sit down and write letters to his younger siblings, Karen and Ricardo, the night before the battle of Fallujah began. "Just think about God and we will all be together again," he wrote. "If anything happens to me, just remember I lived my life to the fullest and I'm happy with what I lived." In Karen's letter he added, "Be good and do your best at school. Don't be lazy."[7]

Education and hard work—these were two things Sergeant Peralta valued. After completing elementary and junior high school in Tijuana, his family moved to San Diego, where he graduated from Morse High School before taking classes at San Diego City College. It was in 1997 while attending high school that he first wanted to enter the military. But his pride in America and love for his new country were not enough to overcome his noncitizen status. If his dream of becoming a U.S. marine were to be realized, he would have to wait until 2000 to receive his green card. And that's exactly what he did.

The very day he became a legal resident, Rafael Peralta enlisted to become a U.S. marine. In so doing, he joined the long, proud history of the U.S. Marine Corps. In all he did, it was that lineage, that long line of heroic marines who had come before him, that Peralta strived to honor, especially that fateful day in Fallujah, Iraq.

Fallujah. For most Americans, the very name conjures up the ghastly images that shocked the nation on March 31, 2004. It was a scene reminiscent of the *Black Hawk Down* incident in Mogadishu, Somalia. The bodies of four American contractors—individuals who had gone to Iraq to help citizens rebuild their nation—had been torched and dragged through the streets of Fallujah before being hung from ropes tied atop a Euphrates River bridge as mobs of cheering, laughing Saddam loyalists, both young and old, danced in jubilant celebration.

That the city of Fallujah would become the most difficult battle waged in Iraq was hardly a surprise. Just forty miles from Baghdad, the Sunni city had become a rat's nest filled with Baathists and Islamic fundamentalists seething with anti-American hatred. The most-wanted terrorist in Iraq, Jordanian-born Abu Musab al Zarqawi, had helped turn Fallujah into a base of operations for his terror group. Zarqawi became widely known to the world when he began appearing in videotaped beheadings. But his history of brutality and terror is decades long, prompting the U.S. government to offer a $25-million reward for information leading to his capture.

The horrifying scene of American civilians dangling from the Euphrates River bridge opened up a debate about how to handle Fallujah. Some argued for immediate action. Others supported waiting. Yet with the historic Iraqi elections scheduled for January 30, 2005, everyone agreed that for elections to go forward the battle of Fallujah must be fought and won. The city was filled with jihadists eager to murder the over 8 million Iraqis determined to exercise their newfound freedom. Defeat, therefore, was not an option.

The ten thousand marines, soldiers, and Iraqi troops gearing up for the massive eleven-day assault knew the dangerous nature of urbanized warfare. The city's labyrinth of buildings and alleys would force them to go room to room, building to building, with danger lurking around every corner. The insurgents hidden inside these buildings would be thousands in number and among the fiercest and best trained. They would also be heavily armed. Out of Fallujah's roughly 1,000 city blocks, 203 had weapons caches and ammunition storehouses. Weapons found included 1,000 antitank and antipersonnel mines, 800 mortar rounds, hundreds of grenades, 86 antitank guided missiles, 6,000 artillery and mortar fuses, 87 122mm and 107mm rockets, 328 rounds for recoilless artillery pieces, and uncounted numbers of Kalashnikov automatic rifles and other small arms.[8]

But even more lethal than their weapons were the tactics they employed, which included: using sixty of Fallujah's one hundred mosques as firing stations to shoot at U.S. and Iraqi forces, waving white flags in surrender and then opening fire, booby-trapping just about anything imaginable and planting over 650 improvised explosive devices (IED), using injured enemy fighters as bait to lure U.S. medics to rush to their aid before detonating grenades, threatening to murder those civilians who had yet to flee only to then use them as shields during battle, and using three of Fallujah's hospitals as defensive positions from which to launch RPG and fire machine guns at American and Iraqi forces.[9]

In sum, the battle of Fallujah would be pure hell, and every soldier and marine going in knew it. But more than that, almost to a man, each one believed it was something that needed to be done. Among these was Sergeant Rafael Peralta.

Lance Corporal T. J. Kaemmerer, a combat correspondent who had been attached to Peralta's company and had witnessed his act of extreme valor, recounted the series of events that unfolded that day. Kaemmerer points out that Sergeant Peralta's status as a platoon scout meant he could have chosen to remain in a safer position while the squads of First Platoon entered the insurgent-filled streets of Fallujah. Yet, having interviewed the leathernecks who knew him best, Kaemmerer discovered that according to Peralta's teammates, he would constantly ask whether he could help out by joining a *stack* (the term marines use for a six-man group).[10]

And that was the case on the morning of November 15, 2004, when Sergeant Peralta and his marine brothers woke at daybreak in the abandoned house they had made a home for the night. For seven days now, First Battalion, Third Marines had been embroiled in some of the most brutal fighting of the war. Eliminating the diehard insurgents who longed for martyrdom meant sweeping every house and building, room by room. After wolfing down a breakfast MRE and shaving, the marines of Alpha Company were locked, loaded, and ready to roll.[11]

Lance Corporal Kaemmerer had decided to join Peralta's six-man stack. Marines use two stacks to clear a house. Kaemmerer remembered that he had been placed as the third man of his stack. After they had cleared three houses and were moving to their fourth, however, Kaemmerer said he and Sergeant Peralta switched positions, putting Peralta directly in front of him. Lance Corporal Kaemmerer's powerful account explains, in his own words, the events as he witnessed them unfold:

> When we reached the fourth house, we breached the gate and swiftly approached the building. The first marine in the stack kicked in the front door, revealing a locked door to their front and another at the right.
>
> Kicking in the doors simultaneously, one stack filed swiftly into the room to the front as the other group of marines darted off to the right.
>
> "Clear!" screamed the marines in one of the rooms followed only seconds later by another shout of "Clear!" from the second room. One word told us all we wanted to know about the rooms: There was no one in there to shoot at us.
>
> We found that the two rooms were adjoined and we had another closed door in front of us. We spread ourselves throughout the rooms to avoid a cluster going through the next door.
>
> Two marines stacked to the left of the door as Peralta, rifle in hand, tested the handle. I watched from the middle, slightly off to the right of the room as the handle turned with ease.

Ready to rush into the rear part of the house, Peralta threw open the door.

"*Pop! Pop! Pop!*" Multiple bursts of cap-gun-like sounding AK-47 fire rang throughout the house. Three insurgents with AK-47s were waiting for us behind the door.

Peralta was hit several times in his upper torso and face at point-blank range by the fully automatic 7.62mm weapons employed by three terrorists. Mortally wounded, he jumped into the already cleared, adjoining room, giving the rest of us a clear line of fire through the doorway to the rear of the house.

We opened fire, adding the bangs of M-16A2 service rifles, and the deafening, rolling cracks of a squad automatic weapon, or "SAW," to the already nerve-racking sound of the AKs. One marine was shot through the forearm and continued to fire at the enemy.

I fired until marines closer to the door began to maneuver into better firing positions, blocking my line of fire. Not being an infantryman, I watched to see what those with more extensive training were doing.

I saw four marines firing from the adjoining room when a yellow, foreign-made, oval-shaped grenade bounced into the room, rolling to a stop close to Peralta's nearly lifeless body.

In an act living up to the heroes of the marine corp's past, such as Medal of Honor recipients Private First Class James LaBelle and Lance Corporal Richard Anderson, Peralta—in his last fleeting moments of consciousness—reached out and pulled the grenade into his body. LaBelle fought on Iwo Jima and Anderson in Vietnam, both died saving their fellow marines by smothering the blast of enemy grenades.

Peralta did the same for all of us in those rooms.

I watched in fear and horror as the other four marines scrambled to the corners of the room and the majority of the blast was absorbed by Peralta's now lifeless body. His selflessness left four other marines with only minor injuries from smaller fragments of the grenade.

During the fight, a fire was sparked in the rear of the house. The flames were becoming visible through the door.

The decision was made by the marine in charge of the squad to evacuate the injured marines from the house, regroup, and return to finish the fight and retrieve Peralta's body.

We quickly ran for shelter, three or four houses up the street, in a house that had already been cleared and was occupied by the squad's platoon.

As Staff Sergeant Jacob M. Murdock took a count of the marines coming back, he found it to be one man short and demanded to know the whereabouts of the missing marine.

"Sergeant Peralta! He's dead! He's f_____ dead," screamed Lance Corporal Adam Morrison, a machine gunner with the squad, as he came around a corner. "He's still in there. We have to go back."

The ingrained code marines have of never leaving a man behind drove the next few moments. Within seconds, we headed back to the house not knowing what we may encounter yet ready for another round.

I don't remember walking back down the street or through the gate in front of the house, but walking through the door the second time, I prayed that we wouldn't lose another brother.

We entered the house and met no resistance. We couldn't clear the rest of the house because the fire had grown immensely and the danger of the enemy's weapons cache exploding in the house was increasing by the second.

Most of us provided security while Peralta's body was removed from the house. We carried him back to our rally point and upon returning were told that the other marines who went to support us encountered and killed the three insurgents inside the house.

Later that night, while I was thinking about the day's somber events, Corporal Richard A. Mason, an infantryman with Headquarters Platoon, who, in the short time I was with the company, became a good friend, told me, "You're still here, don't forget that. Tell your kids, your grandkids, what Sergeant Peralta did for you and the other marines today."[12]

Had he been able, Sergeant Rafael Peralta would have probably told us the same thing that so many of the individuals we were privileged to speak with said: "I wasn't the only one out there; I was just doing my job; I was surrounded by heroes, my marine brothers, men whose hearts contain the same amount of love for their friends and freedom." But Sergeant Peralta's actions had expressed more than his words ever could.

"Fallujah is going to be right up there among the most successful battles in Iraq," said Major Tom Davis, forty-five, of St. Cloud, Minnesota. "It's where the rubber meets the road. That is where our heroes did their best."[13] Winning had come at a horrible cost, claiming the lives of seventy-one American soldiers and marines. However, a consensus among the men who fought in Fallujah, military analysts, and experts has emerged: The victory in Fallujah proved pivotal in paving the way for the historic Iraqi elections two months later. American and Iraqi forces eliminated an estimated sixteen hundred insurgents and wounded and captured hundreds more. Today, with reconstruction still underway, military leaders have declared Fallujah one of the safest cities in Iraq.

General John Satler, commander of the marine expeditionary force that waged the battle of Fallujah, said that the city will become a model for how democracy can take hold in Iraq. While stressing that much hard work remains ahead, Satler said that the victory not only was an essential component to holding open and free democratic elections but also provided a great psychological boost.[14] And while morale for the mission's success was high, the task of burying the marines who had died would weigh heavy on each heart, especially for the families.

When Sergeant Peralta's body was returned home to the States, he received a hero's funeral. The event would be emotional. The explosion from the blast had been so violent that his family members had to rely on the tattoo on his shoulder in order to properly identify him.[15] On November 23, 2004, Peralta, twenty-five, was buried at the Fort Rosecrans National Cemetery in San Diego, California, following a moving funeral mass at the Marine Corps Recruit Depot.

For his marine brothers, it was a time for grateful reflection and remembrance. "He saved half my fire team," said Corporal Brannon Dyer, twenty-seven, of Blairsville, Georgia. Platoon mate Corporal Rob Rogers, twenty-two, of Tallahassee, Florida, agreed: "He'd stand up for his marines to an insane point."[16]

But for Peralta's mother, Rosa, and his siblings, Icela, Ricardo, and Karen, the death of their beloved Rafael had stirred up a range of emotions. They had experienced so much loss and tragedy in such a short span of time. It had only been three years since the death of Rafael's father. And then, on the eve of Rafael and Maritca's wedding, they had lost Maritca's mother. So when Maritca herself was killed in a truck accident while traveling to bury her own mother, it had seemed as if life couldn't deal the family another tragedy. But it had.

In a Thanksgiving Day closing segment on *ABC News*, Icela expressed her internal struggle: "It's just hard, because I know he saved a lot of people. And it's something that I should be proud of. But I'm kind of hurt because I needed him. I needed him over here."[17]

Sergeant Peralta's younger sister, Karen, thirteen, was left to confront life without a father and now her older brother. She worried that his life and legacy would soon be forgotten: "I know that right now, people are really nice and everything. When it's going to be like, one year or two years, they are going to forget about him. . . . Right now they are giving medals to my mom for everything. But I know that when it comes to later on, they are going to forget him, they're gonna forget about him."[18]

Karen Peralta's worries might soon subside, however. While Sergeant Rafael Peralta has already been awarded a Purple Heart, he is currently under consideration to join Sergeant First Class Paul Ray Smith as the only other individual in the War on Terror to be awarded the Medal of Honor. Indeed, Sergeant Peralta seems to be on the mind of President George W. Bush quite often these days, as he has mentioned the heroic marine in a number of his public appearances and speeches.

During his 2005 Memorial Day radio address, for example, President Bush said, "Rafael Peralta also understood that America faces dangerous enemies, and he knew the sacrifices required to defeat them." On June 16, 2005, at the National Hispanic Prayer Breakfast in Washington, D.C., the president paid tribute to Sergeant Peralta again:

> Finally, we see the love of neighbor in tens of thousands of Hispanics who serve America and the cause of freedom. One of these was an immigrant from Mexico named Rafael Peralta. The day after Rafael got his green card, he enlisted in the Marine Corps. Think about that. While serving in Iraq, this good sergeant wrote a letter to his younger brother. He said, "Be proud of being an American. Our father came to this country, became a citizen because it was the right place for our family to be." Shortly after writing that letter, Sergeant Peralta used his own body to cover a grenade an enemy soldier had rolled into a roomful of marines.
>
> This prayer breakfast, we remember the sacrifices of honorable and good folks like Sergeant Peralta, who have shown their love of neighbor by giving their life for freedom.

For the marines inside that room in Fallujah—the men for whom Sergeant Peralta gave the last full measure of devotion—they will unquestionably do as the president suggests: They will remember. For the Peralta family, it is hard to imagine that a day will pass when thoughts of their hero will not fill their hearts and minds. And yet even if Sergeant Rafael

Peralta, a man who signed up to serve his country the first chance he could, is awarded the Medal of Honor, his thirteen-year-old sister's question will linger: Will Americans forget?

Or will they celebrate the life of a young man who awoke each morning to the sight of his boot camp graduation picture, the Bill of Rights, and the Declaration of Independence? A young man whose last words written to his little brother echo the wisdom of the generation of heroes that came before him: "Be proud of being an American."

AFTERWORD

HAVE THE MAINSTREAM MEDIA
IGNORED OUR HEROES?

Why do media refuse to report anything positive about the War on Terrorism?

Why haven't we heard more about the heroic actions of our military serving in Afghanistan and Iraq?

Why are the liberal media so intensely hostile to the efforts of our soldiers, sailors, airmen, and marines?

If you've thought or asked similar questions since the War on Terror began, you're not alone. For over three years now, we've listened and nodded in agreement as countless coworkers, churchgoers, talk-radio callers, friends, and family have expressed frustration with what appears to be the determination of some media to ignore the stories of heroism and hope coming out of Afghanistan and Iraq. It sometimes seems that some in the mainstream media have followed a single rule when reporting on our military and the War on Terror: *all negative, all the time.*

To be sure, as General William Tecumseh Sherman famously observed, "War is hell." And so we agree that it is important for the media to depict the awful human costs war exacts: Children *do* cry when mom or dad leaves for battle; GIs *do* tragically lose limbs; innocent civilians *are* accidentally killed; and just as with the generations of soldiers, sailors, airmen, and marines before them, Americans have and will continue to die while protecting and defending freedom. The media have a right—indeed, a responsibility—to remind us of these realities. And as they do, it is fitting that we mourn deeply and renew our dedication to pray for what every human heart longs for: peace.

But after years of watching and reading coverage of the War on Terror, many citizens, including us, have been awestruck by the lack of balance and objectivity exercised by many American reporters and news executives. The dearth of hopeful or heroic stories reported has given viewers a lopsided perspective. It seems many in the media are willing to highlight only the actions of service members who can be portrayed as either victims or villains.

Case in point: the *New York Times* and its seeming preoccupation with the Abu Ghraib prison abuses. To date, the *New York Times* has devoted over fifty front-page articles to the story! And of course, what the *New York Times* reports, television news and smaller papers quickly pick up. Currently, not a single individual chronicled in this book—some of the most highly decorated members of the U.S. military—has received a front-page story in the *New York Times* devoted to his or her valorous actions. Even when Sergeant First Class Paul R. Smith was awarded the Medal of Honor, the best the *New York Times* could muster was a story buried on page 13.[1] Why? Is it too much to ask to run a positive front-page article, say, once a month?

Reasonable people can disagree about the War on Terror and its execution. After all, in a democratic society, such debate is important and healthy. Yet one thing of which there can be no debate is the heroism, sincerity, and sacrifice of the men and women of our armed forces. They are the best among us. A nation that ignores or, worse, *attacks* its heroes erodes and disparages its own ethos.

One must ask: How far has the journalistic bar been lowered when the chief news executive of CNN, Eason Jordan, has to resign after allegedly claiming that it was official U.S. military policy to deliberately kill American journalists? We use the word *allegedly* because videotape of the closed-door panel at the World Economic Forum in Davos, Switzerland, has remained hidden from the public. Yet according to liberal Democratic Congressman Barney Frank, who was in the audience and heard Mr. Eason's remarks, "It sounded like he was saying it was official military policy to take out journalists." The congressman added, "He [Eason] did say he was talking about cases of deliberate killing."[2]

Eason would, of course, file the obligatory "clarification" of his comments and apologize for any "misunderstanding." The outrageous claim, totally unsupported by evidence of any kind, was the kind of paranoid "blame America first" conspiracy theory one might expect from a tabloid magazine, not a top news executive at CNN. Thus, Eason resigned.

However, CNN's Mr. Eason and the *New York Times* aren't the only ones who consistently find fault with the U.S. military. Not by far. Peter Arnett, formerly of NBC and *National Geographic*, was a name many Americans became familiar with during coverage of the 1991 Gulf War. Older viewers knew him well before that, as Arnett, seventy, had received a Pulitzer Prize for his coverage of the Vietnam War. Therefore it came as a surprise to many observers when, in April 2003, Mr. Arnett granted an interview to state-controlled Iraqi TV. Worse still, not only had Mr. Arnett injected his personal opinions into his interview with Saddam's propaganda machine, to many, Arnett's opinions also seemed designed to stoke the flames of Iraqi resistance.

"The first war plan has failed because of Iraqi resistance," Mr. Arnett declared on Saddam's television network. "Now they [U.S. military] are trying to write another war plan. Clearly, the American war planners misjudged the determination of the Iraqi forces."[3]

In the wake of being fired from NBC and *National Geographic* for his actions, like Mr. Jordan, Mr. Arnett issued an apology for having granted an interview to Saddam Hussein's TV station. Soon thereafter, however, he was quickly hired by the British tabloid, *The Daily Mirror*. But by then the damage had already been done. One wonders what Mr. Arnett's editorializing must have done for the morale of Saddam's forces and the terrorists who had seen an award-winning veteran reporter of American wars declare that our men and women in uniform had "failed."

Sadly, the eagerness to cast the U.S. military and the War on Terror in a negative light is not atypical among today's liberal media. But it is also true that some major news organizations and reporters have featured substantive stories acknowledging the heroic actions of our military. In the interest of fairness and balance, we have made a good-faith effort to integrate these reports where they exist. Two examples we found to be especially representative are Steve Fainaru's reporting for the *Washington Post* on the actions of Staff Sergeant Timothy Nein, Sergeant Leigh Ann Hester, and Specialist Jason Mike, and the reporting on Sergeant First Class Paul Smith by Alex Leary of the *St. Petersburg Times*.

Pockets of military-friendly television reporting exist as well. For example, CNN's Lou Dobbs makes a point of featuring outstanding members of the U.S. military during his "Heroes" segment. Chris Matthews—hardly a conservative—makes a point of honoring servicemen and women on his program, *Hardball*. Sean Hannity of FOX News's *Hannity & Colmes*, of course, remains one of the strongest supporters of our troops (as several individuals we interviewed told us), even going as far as organizing and hosting Freedom Fest rallies around the country to encourage and honor our soldiers, sailors, airmen, marines, and their families. With the notable exception of FOX News, however, it is often the local hometown television stations and newspapers that cover the awarding of a medal, not national news organizations.

Like Mr. Jordan and Mr. Arnett, several nationally recognized reporters continue to allow their political prejudices to supersede their journalistic integrity. In the process, Americans have been forced to sit and listen while media outlets use their global megaphones to attack and belittle not just their commander in chief but also the sacrifices of the 150,000 brave heroes still risking their lives to defend freedom.

Brent Bozell, president of the Media Research Center, has catalogued hundreds of audacious quotes from leading reporters and media executives. Consider the following:

- "The reason that the World Trade Center got hit is because there are a lot of people living in abject poverty out there who don't have any hope for a better life. . . . I think they [the nineteen hijackers] were brave at the very least."

—AOL Time Warner Vice Chairman and CNN founder Ted Turner in February 11 remarks at Brown University, as reported by Gerald Carbone in the February 12, 2002, *Providence Journal*. The next day, Turner issued a statement: "The attacks of September 11 were despicable acts. I in no way meant to convey otherwise."

• Headline: Our Soldiers in Iraq Aren't Heroes.

"We should not bestow the mantle of heroism on all of them [American men and women in uniform] for simply being where we sent them. Most are victims, not heroes."

—CBS News *60 Minutes* commentator Andy Rooney, writing for *The Buffalo News*, April 12, 2004.

• "We all know that one man's terrorist is another man's freedom fighter and that Reuters upholds the principle that we do not use the word terrorist. . . . To be frank, it adds little to call the attack on the World Trade Center a terrorist attack."

—Steven Jukes, global head of news for Reuters News Service, in an internal memo cited by the *Washington Post*'s Howard Kurtz in a September 24, 2001, article.

• "What drives American civilians to risk death in Iraq? In this economy it may be, for some, the only job they can find."

—Dan Rather denigrating the men and women of the armed forces by suggesting their decision to serve their nation was a last resort during the *CBS Evening News* on March 31, 2004, the day four American civilians were killed and mutilated in Fallujah, Iraq.

• "The other day, while taking a break by the Al-Hamra Hotel pool . . . I was accosted by an American magazine journalist

of serious accomplishment and impeccable liberal creden-
tials. . . . She came to the point. Not only had she 'known'
the Iraq war would fail but she considered it essential that it
did so because this would ensure that the 'evil' George W.
Bush would no longer be running her country. Her editors
back on the East Coast were giggling, she said, over what a
disaster Iraq had turned out to be. 'Lots of us talk about how
awful it would be if this worked out.' "

—British journalist Toby Harnden, a reporter for the *London Daily
Telegraph*, in an article published in the May 15, 2004, edition of *The
Spectator*, a British-based weekly, recounting a conversation at a
Baghdad hotel.

• "Like beauty, freedom is a perception that lies in the eye of
the beholder, and we ignore other nations' versions at our
peril. The most dangerous perception of all may be that
one's own side has an exclusive claim to either the truth or
patriotism."

—CBS News foreign correspondent, Allen Pizzey, preaching moral
relativism on CBS's *Sunday Morning*, October 14, 2001.

• **Diane Sawyer:** "I read this morning that he's [Saddam Hus-
sein] also said the love that the Iraqis have for him is so
much greater than anything Americans feel for their president because he's been loved for thirty-five years, he says,
the whole thirty-five years."

Dan Harris in Baghdad: "He is one to point out quite frequently that he is part of a historical trend in this country of
restoring Iraq to its greatness, its historical greatness. He
points out frequently that he was elected with a hundred
percent margin recently."

—ABC's *Good Morning America*, March 7, 2003.

- "I decided to put on my flag pin tonight—first time. . . . I put it on to remind myself that not every patriot thinks we should do to the people of Baghdad what bin Laden did to us."

  —Bill Moyers on PBS's *Now*, February 28, 2003.

As reprehensible as these quotes are, it is important to remember that these are not the banal protestations of the usual gaggle of American detractors like Barbara Streisand, Whoopi Goldberg, or Michael Moore, individuals whose rants are easily swatted away. These are some of our nation's *leading journalistic lights*, people whose words ricochet around the globe and often set the terms of debate for world leaders on issues of global concern.

Again, we believe that a free and open press remains one of the pillars of a democratic society; our argument isn't that these reporters aren't entitled to their personal opinions, or that they shouldn't cover the tragedies of warfare, or even that they shouldn't express their views. Rather, our concern is that while Eason Jordan, Peter Arnett, the *New York Times*, and the scores of others in the mainstream media enthusiastically decry the U.S. military and the War on Terror, the inspirational and heroic actions of an entire generation of soldiers, sailors, airmen, and marines have gone unnoticed.

It isn't that liberal reporters are incapable of singling out the actions of U.S. soldiers and featuring them prominently. They do it all the time. The problem is that their knee-jerk response when covering the U.S. military is to portray members of our armed forces only as victims or villains. According to *National Review* editor, Kate O'Beirne, the three major networks have run over two hundred stories on the seven disgraced soldiers involved at Abu Ghraib, thus pounding the image into our collective memory and the memories of millions of Muslims around the globe.[4] Thus when we hear the words *Abu Ghraib* and *dog leash*, our minds instantly snap to the now-infamous picture of Army Private First Class Lynndie England tethered to an enemy prisoner.

But what about the words *battle of Tarmiya*? Do you experience a similar connection to a Marine Sergeant Marco Martínez? Try another one: *burning tank* and *Najaf*? Does the image of Army Sergeant Javier Camacho leaping on a flaming tank before muscling open a jammed tank turret and rescuing Private First Class Adam Small instantly come to mind? Or what about *the Saddam Canal Bridge* and *lifesaving valor*? Does your mind's eye immediately paint a picture of Navy Hospitalman Third Class Luis E. Fonseca, Jr.? Or how about *Qala-i-Jangi fortress* and *Army Lieutenant Colonel Mark Mitchell*? Does your mind leap to thoughts of the David versus Goliath–like battle between Mitchell and his fifteen Special Forces soldiers up against five hundred Taliban and al Qaeda fighters engaged in an uprising inside a nineteenth-century fortress, a battle that led to the repatriation of CIA agent Johnny "Mike" Spann, the first combat death in the War on Terror, and the capture of the so-called American Taliban, John Walker Lindh?

Of course not.

The reason: None of these men meets the victim or villain standard, thus the liberal media find their stories uninteresting and unworthy of coverage. After all, these men are heroes, and if you believe, as many in the mainstream media seem to, that concepts like "good" and "evil" are subjective and up for interpretation, then the word *hero* is meaningless. And that's the problem.

Many in the media find words like *hero* too black and white, too judgmental, too certain of our nation's purpose and essential goodness. In a world where there is no distinction between good and evil, *by definition*, heroes cease to exist. That's why the earlier quote from the head of Reuter's News Service, one of the largest and most powerful news organizations in the world, is so revealing. It illustrates that reporters of such ilk draw no distinction between the terrorists and our own soldiers. "After all," they reason, "one man's freedom fighter is another man's terrorist." And since accounts of military valor do not comport with the strong liberal bias found in many media organizations, you can be sure these stories of valor and heroism will not be retold, at least not by the mainstream media.

That is why we wrote this book: to pay tribute to the 2.4 million men and women of our armed forces and their families. We wrote it to *honor the unsung heroes in the War on Terror*.

No single book could even begin to repay the sacrifices made by the American military and their families. Indeed, one of the greatest struggles we faced was in selecting the stories to recount. There are literally *thousands* from which to choose, and some individuals' stories (mostly Navy SEALS) we were prevented from telling for security reasons. Yet the individuals included in this volume not only are some of the most highly decorated in the U.S. military, they also are indicative of the hundreds of thousands of men and women who serve alongside them. Every hero we interviewed or researched was quick to share credit with his teammates or to suggest others we should profile. To a person, each one said, "I'm not a hero. I was just doing my job." We respectfully disagree.

In our eyes, and in the eyes of the overwhelming majority of the American people, *every* man or woman who honorably wears a uniform is worthy of our deepest respect and gratitude. We do not share Mr. Rooney's belief that Americans join the U.S. military because they are "victims" with no abilities, skills, or opportunities. Indeed, perhaps Mr. Rooney would do well to remember that while he was drafted into the Army in 1941, today's young people *choose* to join, often forgoing attractive options to do other things or make greater sums of money. The stories contained in this book reveal that most who join the military do so to serve a purpose larger than themselves.

The grand irony, of course, is that without these heroes, the Eason Jordans, Peter Arnetts, and Andy Rooneys of the world would be unable to express their personal views so freely and openly. But as Master Sergeant William "Calvin" Markham, put it, "When I hear that kind of thing, honestly, it makes me glad, because it means those individuals have the freedom to think and say what they wish. . . . The media are sometimes a little like how some people are when watching a NASCAR race; they're waiting for the crash. They're waiting for the bad thing to happen. But basically I think they're armchair quarterbacks. They don't see the bigger picture of what we're trying to do."

We agree.

And fortunately, a new breed of journalists—Internet bloggers—are beginning to challenge the mainstream media.

Some of the best information and stories can be found in the vibrant world of military blogs (often called milblogs). These websites are often generated from firsthand accounts taken directly from GIs on the ground in Afghanistan and Iraq. This new breed of journalism is still in its infancy, but we believe milblogs offer military personnel, their families, and civilians a view of the U.S. military that is distinct from the one offered by the mainstream media. We remain optimistic that their presence and "reach" will continue to grow as the liberal mainstream media's influence continues to wane.

As Hugh Hewitt points out, military blogs, such as The Mudville Gazette (www.mudvillegazette.com), Black Five (www.blackfive.net), Chief Wiggles (www.chiefwiggles.blog-city.com), Smash (www.lt-smash.us), and others like Home of Heroes (www.homeofheroes.com) are leading the way in revolutionizing the access citizens have to information obtained from sources on the ground who, unlike many in the mainstream media, are not hostile to the U.S. military.[5]

Yet regardless of whether the barrage of negativity from mainstream media continues, the actions of our military have resulted in breathtaking, historic changes that are beginning to transform the world and pave the way for increased peace and security. Looking over the arc of history, every fight for human freedom has been opposed by ruthless and determined enemies. Therefore we can expect that the road that lies ahead will continue to be marked by danger, setbacks, and, tragically, the loss of the most brave and honorable among us. As President Bush told the world just nine days after September 11, "Americans should not expect one battle, but a lengthy campaign, unlike any other we have ever seen."

While much work remains to be done, it is essential that we take stock of all that has already been accomplished. For over three years now, 150,000 American airmen, soldiers, sailors, and marines have been engaged in one of the most historic transformations the Middle East has ever seen. In Afghanistan, for example, young American men and women routed the Taliban, destroyed al Qaeda terrorist training camps, uncovered and destroyed thousands of tons of lethal weapons, liberated a people, and ushered in the first democratic elections in Afghan history. Ten million Afghans voted, including women who had been beaten and oppressed for generations. Women took off their burkhas, men shaved their beards, music filled the air, children flew kites (an activity once illegal under the Taliban), and a democratic constitution and system of government was established.

Given Operation Enduring Freedom's continued success, it is easy to forget the strident and often vicious attacks that some in politics and the media launched during the time leading up to the routing of the Taliban and al Qaeda terrorists in Afghanistan. As acclaimed military historian Victor Davis Hanson writes, "We forget now the furor over hitting back in Afghanistan—a quagmire in the words of *New York Times* columnists R. W. Apple and Maureen Dowd; a 'terrorist campaign' against Muslims, according to Representative Cynthia McKinney; a 'silent genocide' in Noam Chomsky's ranting."[6]

Then came Iraq. Mass graves filled with thousands of bodies were unearthed, torture chambers were razed, and enormous stockpiles of weapons were uncovered. The chief weapon of mass destruction himself, Saddam Hussein, the tyrant responsible for the slaughter of over 300,000 individuals was captured peacefully after having been found hiding in a spider hole nine miles from his hometown of Tikrit. After three long decades of his murderous reign was ended, just as promised, the Iraqi elections went forward. And when they did, over 8 million Iraqis, including millions of women, defied the terrorists and suicide bombers as they exercised their right to vote.

Of the 275 members of the transitional national assembly, 80 representatives were women. The images of millions of smiling Iraqis and ink-stained fingers—the equivalent of America's "I Voted" sticker—were so undeniably hopeful, that in a rare moment of apparent concession, even the *New York Times* seemed to give the administration credit in a March 1, 2005, editorial: "The Bush administration is entitled to claim a healthy share of the credit for many of these advances."

On December 15, 2005, when it was time for Iraqis to head to the polls to elect their parliamentary government, Iraqis, both Shiite and Sunni alike, streamed to the polling stations in what even the Associated Press had to admit was "one of the largest and freest elections in the Arab world." Voting lines were so long, in fact, that some polling stations were forced to extend their hours to accommodate the waves of eager Iraqis. As Buthana Mehdi, an Iraqi schoolteacher, told one CNN reporter, "It's a special day. It's the beginning of our new life."

But as the president and others are quick to mention, it is the men and women of our military and the people of Iraq who deserve credit not only for the historic changes in the

Middle East—events that have begun to spark democratic movements across the region—but also for the continued defense of our way of life.

Does America remain vulnerable? Absolutely. Will the War on Terror demand continued sacrifice? Unquestionably. Yet as the brave men and women of the U.S. military march forward to defend freedom and fulfill their duty, so too must we fulfill ours: to pause and offer thanks to those who protect us.

The challenge, of course, is that citizens can only know that which they read in their newspapers and watch on TV news. This "monopoly of perspective" has led some historians to question whether America would have won past wars had today's media been around to cover them. Their answers are not so sanguine. In an interview with Tim Russert, Pulitzer Prize–winning historian David McCullough stated that if today's media had been around in 1776, George Washington could have never have won the Revolutionary War: "I have to say too if that war had been covered . . . by the media, and the country had seen now horrible the conditions were, how badly things were being run by the officers, and what a very serious soup we were in, I think that would have been it."

The liberal mainstream media know that Mr. McCullough is absolutely correct, and they pride themselves in their ability to exert power and influence over American public opinion. Yet we as citizens should not feel paralyzed; there is much Americans can and must do. We must stand with those who consider it a privilege to defend us. We must reach out to their families and children, especially those who have lost loved ones in combat. We must support them in our communities

and through our service groups. We must thank them when
we pass them on the street or in the airport. And above all, we
must always remember the great and enduring lesson American history teaches: "Ours would not be the land of the free if
it were not also the home of the brave."

ACKNOWLEDGMENTS

Quite literally, so many individuals gave so much to make this book possible. First and foremost, we want to extend our most sincere thanks to the soldiers, sailors, airmen, and marines discussed in this book and their families. Your heroism is matched only by your humility. The time many of you spent with us and the intimacy of the information you shared moved us deeply. Thank you for sharing some of the most hellish and hopeful remembrances of your lives. You lived the moments. Thank you for helping us write about them. Specifically, we wish to thank: Marine First Sergeant Justin D. LeHew; Navy Hospital Corpsman Third Class Luis E. Fonseca, Jr.; Air Force Master Sergeant William "Calvin" Markham; Marine Sergeant Marco A. Martínez; Air Force Staff Sergeant Stephen A. Achey; Marine Captain Brian Chontosh; Marine Corporal Armand McCormick; Marine Corporal Robert Kerman; Army Lieutenant Colonel Mark E. Mitchell; Army Sergeant Micheaux Sanders; Army Captain William T. Pohlmann.

Contacting the individuals profiled and others was only possible due to the heavy lifting performed by an impressive cast of military public affairs officers who approached *Home of the Brave* as a labor of love. We wish to thank the following individuals for their time and attention to even the smallest requests: Director for Army Public Affairs, New York, Bruce E. Zielsdorf; MAJ Robert E. Gowan PAO,

U.S. Army Special Forces Command; LCDR Stephen C. Elgin, MSC, USN; CDR Dave E. Gibson, MSC, USN, Commanding Officer, Second Medical Battalion, Second FSSG; CDR Paula McClure, MSC, USN; CDR Dave E. Gibson, MSC, USN, FACHE; Mr. Shane L. Darbonne, USMC; GYSGT Kristine Scarber, USMC; CPT Jeff Landis, USMC; CPT Juliet R Chelkowski, USMC; CPT Carrie C. Batson, USMC; MAJ David C. Andersen, USMC; CPT. Jason Medina, USAF; First LT Gary E. Arasin, Jr., USAF.

We are deeply grateful to our friend Sean Hannity for reviewing early drafts of the manuscript and offering his insights and suggestions. Also, we would like to recognize L. Brent Bozell and the Media Research Center for the important work they do in keeping a watchful eye on the media.

The concept and title of this book sprang from the brow of Hoover Fellow Peter Schweizer. He has been a coauthor with each of us on other books and remains a dear friend to us both. We remain indebted to him for his fertile mind and ironclad support.

Our literary agent, Joseph Brendan Vallely, is the consummate professional. His twenty years in the New York literary game continue to serve us well. And for that—and much more—we remain grateful. Likewise, our editor at Forge, Bob Gleason, brought a wealth of experience and passion to this project for which we are most appreciative. He immediately understood the need for a book like ours and marshaled the forces necessary to bring it to fruition. Bob's right hand at Forge, Eric Raab, was tireless in his effort to make sure that this book was produced in a timely and professional manner. Ensuring that the book was seen was the work of publicists David Moench and Bob Angelotti, both of whom define professionalism. Also, we would like to thank our publisher, Tom Doherty. Despite his frenetic schedule, he was never too busy to take time to offer encouragement and support.

During the writing of the book, we benefited from the steadfast support of the Forbes family; Bainbridge College; Patrick A. Smith; Dick Wirthlin; Yusuf and Nicole Haidermota; Phil Reyes; Jack Weisser; Creighton and Jane Buie; Dr. and Mrs. Wynton L. Hall; Holly, Leslie, and Isabella Hall; and Mr. and Mrs. William Dellinger.

Without the extraordinarily talented Kay Leisz, who has served as Caspar Weinberger's executive assistant going back to the Pentagon days, this book would have been all but impossible. We thank her.

Finally, we express our unending gratitude and affection for our wives, Jane Weinberger and Katie Hall. Your support, beauty, and courage inspire us daily. We are better men because of you.

NOTES

CHAPTER 1

1. Elena Arnold, "Bravery Breeds Honor, Praise," *The Press-Enterprise*, May 7, 2004, p. B01.
2. Ibid.
3. Corporal Jeremy M. Vought, "3/5 Marines Awarded for Heroism," *Marine Corps News, MCB Camp Pendleton*, May 13, 2004.

CHAPTER 2

1. Mary Kennedy, "Brave Soldier 'Gave My Son His Life Back,'" *USA Today*, December 31, 2003, p. 12A. Mrs. Kennedy's letter to the editor appeared following our Christmas 2003 op-ed in *USA Today*, wherein we recounted Sergeant First Class Camacho's actions.
2. Ibid.
3. Sean D. Naylor, "Quick-thinking NCOs Rescue Soldiers from Burning Tank," *Army Times*, March 28, 2003.
4. Kim Angelastro, "Fort Stewart Soldier Awarded Silver Star," WTOC 11, October 24, 2003. http://www.wtoctv.com/global/story.asp?s=1496591.
5. Ibid.
6. Pfc. Benjamin T. Brody, "Cav. Soldier Receives Silver Star," *The Frontline*, October 30, 2003.

7. Ibid.
8. John Schneider, "Hero Prizes Letter from a Mom over Medal," *Lansing State Journal*, October 29, 2003.
9. Ibid.
10. Mary Kennedy, "Brave Soldier."

CHAPTER 4

1. Orlando Salinas, "Air Force's Special Team Readies for War," September 4, 2002, FOX News.
2. Tech. Sergeant Ginger Schreitmueller, "Combat Controller Makes History with CAS Operations in OEF," *Public Affairs Press Release*, NFNS 02-XX.
3. Ibid.
4. Ibid.
5. Gregg K. Kakesako, "Airman Awarded Silver Star," *Honolulu Star Bulletin*, December 14, 2004. http://starbulletin.com/2004/12/19/news/story6.html.
6. Tech. Sergeant Ginger Schreitmueller, "Combat Controller."

CHAPTER 5

1. William Weir, "Town Honors One of Its Soldiers for Valor in War," *Hartford Courant*, October 13, 2003, p. B1.
2. Ibid.
3. Jesse Hamilton, "Cromwell Grad Gets Silver Star," *Hartford Courant*, September 13, 2003, p. B3.
4. Ibid.
5. William Weir, "Town Honors One of Its Soldiers."
6. Spc. Bill Putnam, "Silver Star Awards Mark Sept. 11th Anniversary," *Army News Service*, September 12, 2003.

7. Ibid.

8. Jesse Hamilton, "Cromwell Grad Gets Silver Star."

CHAPTER 6

1. *U.S. Fed News*, "11th MEU Marine Awarded Navy Cross for Legendary Day During OIF," July 29, 2004.

2. John Keegan, *The Iraq War* (New York: Alfred A. Knopf, 2004), p. 149.

3. Sgt. Andrew W. Miller, "VMX-22 Marine Recognized for Lifesaving Efforts," *Rotovue*, 44, 5 (March 9, 2005): 3.

4. Cpl. Matthew S. Richards/11th Marine Expeditionary Unit, "Marine Receives Navy Cross," *U.S. Department of Defense News About the War on Terrorism*, August 6, 2004.

CHAPTER 7

1. Danna Sue Walker, "A Hero's Tale," *The Tulsa World*, November 28, 2004, p. D8.

2. Rich Connell and Robert J. López, "Deadly Day for Charlie Company," *Los Angeles Times*, August 26, 2003, p. A1.

3. Ibid.

4. Jim Axelrod, "War Casts Shadow in 'Swingtown,'" CBSNEWS.com, May 11, 2004. http://www.cbsnews.com/stories/2004/05/11/eveningnews/printable616783.shtml.

5. Raymond L. Applewhite and Eric Schwab, "Corpsman Awarded Navy Cross," *Navy Newsstand*, August 12, 2004 [story number: NNS040812-05]. http://www.news.navy.mil/search/display.asp?story_id=14707.

CHAPTER 8

1. Jessica Inigo, " 'Other Soldiers . . . Were Depending On Us,' " *Stars and Stripes*, June 14, 2004.

2. Jason L. Austin, "Two USAREUR Officers Rated Best in Army," USAREUR Public Affairs News Release, March 8, 2005.

3. Scott Wilson, "Over 60 Days, Troops Suppressed an Uprising," *The Washington Post*, June 26, 2004, p. A01.

4. Specialist Rebecca Burt, "V Corps Tanker Who Earned Silver Star for Heroism in Iraq Says 'Fuss' Over His Actions 'Feels Weird,' " V Corps Public Affairs Press Release, December 14, 2004.

5. John C. Moore, "Sadr City: The Armor Pure Assault in Urban Terrain," 2004 U.S. Army Armor Center Report.

6. Ibid.

7. Greg Mitchell, "On Losing a Son, and Saving Others," *Editor & Publisher*, August 18, 2005. http://www.editorandpublisher.com/eandp/columns/pressingissues_display.jsp?vnu_content_id=1001018031.

8. Paul Rockwell, "From Grief to Protest: How Peace Loving Fathers Honor Their Fallen Sons," *In Motion Magazine*, June 11, 2004. http://www.inmotionmagazine.com/opin/pr_fathers.html#Anchor-Bill-49575.

9. Scott Wilson, "Over 60 Days, Troops Suppressed an Uprising."

10. Specialist Rebecca Burt, "V Corps Tanker Who Earned Silver Star for Heroism."

CHAPTER 9

1. Interview, *CNN Live Sunday*, June 19, 2005.

2. Eric Schmitt, "First Woman in Six Decades Gets the Army's Silver Star," *The New York Times*, June 17, 2005, Section A, p. 16. While we are critical of the mainstream media's lack of coverage of our na-

tion's military heroes and the successes and positive stories emanating from Iraq and Afghanistan, it is important to note that Sergeant Hester's Silver Star was widely covered by major media outlets, which we were glad to see. We tried to integrate these reports where appropriate.

3. Sergeant Sara Wood, "Woman Soldier Receives Silver Star for Valor in Iraq," *American Forces Information Service*, June 16, 2005.

4. Tom Bowman, "Woman Honored for Bravery Against Enemy in Iraq Firefight," *The Baltimore Sun*, June 18, 2005, p. 1A.

5. Ibid.

6. Steve Fainaru, "Silver Stars Affirm One Unit's Mettle," *The Washington Post*, June 26, 2005, Section A, p. 1.

7. Sergeant Sara Wood, "Woman Soldier Receives Silver Star for Valor in Iraq."

8. Steve Fainaru, "Silver Stars Affirm One Unit's Mettle."

9. Ibid.

10. Ibid.

11. Army News Service (ARNEWS), "Army Awards MPs for Turning Table on Ambush," June 16, 2005. http://www.4army.mil/ocpa/print.php?story_id_key=7472.

12. Ibid.

13. Steve Fainaru, "Silver Stars Affirm One Unit's Mettle."

14. Ibid.

15. Ibid.

16. Ibid.

17. Army News Service (ARNEWS), "Army Awards MPs for Turning Table on Ambush."

18. Steve Fainaru, "Silver Stars Affirm One Unit's Mettle."

19. Elizabeth Vargas, "Silver Star First Woman to Earn Medal for Gallantry in Action," *ABC News Report*, June 16, 2005.

20. Ibid.

21. James Zambronski, "Medic Awarded Silver Star for Heroism," NBC WAVE Channel 3, November 2, 2005. http://www.wave3 .com/Global/story.asp?S=4062863.

22. Tom Bowman, "Woman Honored for Bravery Against Enemy in Iraq Firefight."

23. Jacqui Goodard, "She's the Shoe Shop War Heroine," *Sunday Mail* (South Australia), June 19, 2005, Foreign, p. 5.

24. Tom Bowman, "Woman Honored for Bravery Against Enemy in Iraq Firefight."

25. John L. Lumpkin, "First Woman Gets Silver Star Since WWII," Associated Press, June 16, 2005.

26. Interview, *CNN Live Sunday,* June 19, 2005.

CHAPTER 10

1. For a comprehensive recounting of Operation Anaconda and the myriad individuals involved, see Sean Naylor, *Not a Good Day to Die: The Untold Story of Operation Anaconda* (New York: Berkley Books, 2005).

CHAPTER 11

1. Lance Corporal Miguel A. Carrasco, Jr., "Navy Cross Marks Fallen Hero's Sacrifice," USMC Press Release, #: 2005531163329, May 21, 2005.

2. Cathy Hodson and Marlene McDowell, "An American Life," *American Association of Nurse Anesthetists NewsBulletin,* July 2004, pp. 8–9.

3. Lance Corporal Miguel A. Carrasco, Jr., "Navy Cross Marks Fallen Hero's Sacrifice."

4. Ibid.

5. Cathy Hodson and Marlene McDowell, "An American Life."

6. Seth Hettena, "Utah Marine Receives Navy Cross for Heroism in Iraq," Associated Press State and Local Wire, April 21, 2005.

7. Lance Corporal Miguel A. Carrasco, Jr., "Navy Cross Marks Fallen Hero's Sacrifice."

8. "Laura Bailey, Honored with a Bronze Star, Cpl. James Wright Sets His Sights on Healing," *Marine Corps Times*, June 4, 2004. http://www.marinetimes.com/story.php?f=1-292925-2981331.php.

9. Ibid.

10. Owen West, "Leadership from the Rear," *Marine Corps Gazette*, September 1, 2005. Note: This outstanding article won the USMC 2005 Leadership Essay Contest. See also, Matthew Dodd, "Capt. Brent Morel, Leading the Charge," *DefenseWatch*, June 27, 2005. http://www.military.com/NewContent/0,13190,Defensewatch_072705_Dodd,00.html.

11. Ibid.

12. Cindy Wolff, "Funeral Is Thursday for Captain Morel," *The Commercial Appeal*, April 14, 2004, p. B1.

13. Ibid.

14. Seth Hettena, "Utah Marine Receives Navy Cross for Heroism in Iraq."

15. Lance Corporal Miguel A. Carrasco, Jr., "Navy Cross Marks Fallen Hero's Sacrifice."

16. Ibid.

17. Fallen Heroes Memorial, http://www.fallenheroesmemorial.com/oif/profiles/morelbrentl.html.

18. Lance Corporal Miguel A. Carrasco, Jr., "Navy Cross Marks Fallen Hero's Sacrifice."

CHAPTER 12

1. Dave Moniz, "Soldier to Be Honored for Valor in Afghanistan," *USA Today*, November 13, 2003. http://www.usatoday.com/news/washington/2003-11-13-mitchell-usat_x.htm.

2. Graham Brink, "A David Wins a Goliath Honor," *St. Petersburg*

Times Online, November 15, 2003. http://www.sptimes.com/2003/11/15/news_pf/Tampabay/A_David_wins_a_goliat.shtml.

3. Evan Thomas, "A Long, Strange Trip to the Taliban," *Newsweek*, December 17, 2001, p. 32.

4. Ibid.

CHAPTER 13

1. Alex Leary, "Son Accepts Medal for Soldier's Sacrifice," *St. Petersburg Times*, April 4, 2005.

2. Allen Mikaelian, *Medal of Honor* (New York: Hyperion, 2002).

3. Ibid.

4. Alex Leary, "The Full Measure of Devotion," *St. Petersburg Times*, January 25, 2004.

5. Ibid.

6. U.S. Army online video tribute: www.army.mil.

7. http://www.sptimes.com/2004/webspecials04/medalofhonor/epilogue.shtml.

8. U.S. Army online video tribute: www.army.mil.

9. Ibid.

10. Ibid.

11. http://www.sptimes.com/2004/webspecials04/medalofhonor/epilogue.shtml.

12. Sergeant Lorie Jewell, "Florida Post Office Takes Name of Medal of Honor Nominee," *Army News Service* (ARNEWS), November 2, 2004. http://www4army.mil/ocpa/print.php?story_id-key=6511.

13. Eric W. Cramer, "Soldiers Relate Smith's Courage Under Fire, Care in Garrison," *Army News Service* (ARNEWS), March 29, 2005. http://www4.army.mil/ocpa/print.php?story_id_key=7087.

14. Ibid.

15. Alex Leary, "The Full Measure of Devotion."

16. Ibid.

17. Ibid.
18. U.S. Army online video tribute: www.army.mil.
19. Ibid.

CHAPTER 14

1. Gordon Trowbridge, "Marine Sacrifices His Life for Others in Grenade Blast," *The Army Times*, November 20, 2004.
2. Jeff Jacoby, "Death of a Marine," *Boston Globe*, May 29, 2005.
3. Caitlin Rother, "Another Tragedy for Grieving Family," *San Diego Union-Tribune*, November 21, 2004, p. B-1.
4. Ibid.
5. Ibid.
6. "Siblings of San Diego Marine Say He Was Prepared for the Chance of Death," Associated Press State and Local Wire, November 22, 2004.
7. Caitlin Rother, "Another Tragedy for Grieving Family."
8. Robert J. Caldwell, "Fallujah Battle Inflicted Crippling Defeat on Terrorists," *San Diego Union-Tribune*, December 5, 2004, p. G-1.
9. Ibid.
10. Gregg K. Kakesako, "Marine Threw Himself on Grenade, Say Comrades," *Honolulu Star-Bulletin*, December 4, 2004. http://starbulletin.com/2004/12/04/news/story4.html.
11. Lance Corporal T. J. Kaemmerer, "A Hero's Sacrifice," December 2, 2004, Story Identification # 2004123102943. http://www.usmc.mil/marinelink/mcn2000.nsf/ac95bc775efc34c685256ab50049d458/4ef649c7ae4cfb6785256fe20049866c?OpenDocument&Highlight=2, Kaemmerer.
12. Ibid.
13. Katrina Kratovac, "Marines: Fallujah Battle a Source of Pride," Associated Press, December 1, 2004.
14. John E. Mulligan, "Marines: Fallujah Turned War for U.S.," *Providence Journal*, March 28, 2005.

15. Jeff Jacoby, "Death of a Marine."

16. Gordon Trowbridge, "Marine Sacrifices His Life for Others in Grenade Blast."

17. Bob Woodruff, "Story of Bravery: Marine Sacrifices His Life for His Platoon," *World News Tonight with Peter Jennings*, November 25, 2004.

18. Ibid.

AFTERWORD

1. Eric Schmitt, "Medal of Honor to Be Awarded to Soldier Killed in Iraq, a First," *New York Times*, March 30, 2005, Section A, p. 13. This article was published prior to the awards ceremony. The day following the ceremony, The *New York Times* ran a piece on the ceremony. It appeared on p. 16.

2. http://www.washingtonpost.com/wp-dyn/articles/A6490-2005 Feb7.html.

3. http://www.cnn.com/2003/WORLD/meast/03/31/sprj.irq.arnett/.

4. Kate O'Beirne, "The Soldiers You Never Hear About," *National Review*, June 14, 2004.

5. Hugh Hewitt, "Rise of the Milblogs," *The Daily Standard*, March 12, 2004. http://www.weeklystandard.com/Content/Public/Articles/000/000/003/840fvgmo.asp.

6. Victor Davis Hanson, "Our Wars Over the War," *National Review Online*, July 15, 2005. http://www.nationalreview.com/hanson/hanson200507150804.asp.

*Unless otherwise noted, direct quotations were obtained through personal interviews by the authors with subjects or colleagues of several of the individuals profiled.

INDEX

ABC News, 230

ABC's *Good Morning America*, 239

Abu Ghraib prison abuses, 241
  New York Times and, 234

Achey, Stephen, 153–54, 154–61,
    161–62
  Silver Star awarded to, 163–64

Air Force Special Tactic group, 68

Al Anbar Province, 167–71

al Qaeda, 71, 161
  Qala-i-Jangi Fortress uprising,
    184–95

al-Sadr, Muqtada, 130

al Zarqawi, Abu Musab, 222

Ali, 41

Alvarez, Maritca, 220–21

Ambush Alley, 105, 114

Anderson, Richard, 226

Apple, R. W., 245

Army National Guard, 140–42

Army Commendation Medal, 151

Arnett, Peter, 235–36, 240

Basilone, John, 14

Beavers, Matthew, 116

Berwald, Louis, 212, 213

Black Five (blog), 146, 244

bloggers, 146, 243–44

Bong, Richard I., 14

Borkowski, Brian, 210

Bozell, Brent, 237

Bradley, Omar, 88

Brenize, First Lieutenant, 98, 103

Brokaw, Tom, 14

Bronze Star, 151

Brooks, Mike, 98

Buffalo News, 238

Bush, George H. W., 7

Bush, George W., 123, 173, 201, 215,
    230–31, 239, 244–45

Camacho, Javier, 39–44, 44–46,
    241
  Najaf, fighting near, 41–44
  Silver Star awarded to, 44–45

Campbell, Timothy, 208

Cantu, Jason, 102

Carbone, Gerald, 237–38

CBS News, 238

CBS Evening News, 238

CBS's *Sunday Morning*, 239

Chief Wiggles (blog), 244

Chomsky, Noam, 245

Chontosh, Brian, 21–25, 31–36
  Highway 1, attacked on, 25–31
  Navy Cross awarded to, 32,
    35–36, 37–38

Chontosh, Colby (daughter), 32

Chontosh, Joy (wife), 32

Chontosh, Sara (daughter), 32

Clark, Colleen, 44

CNN, 235, 246

Coker, Gary, 207–8

Conway, James T., 89

Cooper, Casey, 140, 144, 145,
    147–48
  Bronze Star awarded to, 151

Copeland, Danielle E. (wife),
    168–69

Copeland, Robyn (mother), 172

Copeland, Wille, III, 165–67, 167–71
  Navy Cross awarded to, 166,
    171–72, 176–77

Dahn, Scott, 99

Daly, Daniel, 14

"Dave" (CIA agent), 184, 188

Davis, Tom, 228

Dean, Christopher P., 130, 131,
    132–33

DeLauter, Elizabeth, 208–9

Distinguished Service Cross, 196,
    197, 199

Dobbs, Lou, 237

Dostum, Abdul Rashid, 183,
    184–85, 195

Dowd, Maureen, 245

Dyer, Brannon, 229

England, Gordon R., 123

England, Lynndie, 241

Fainaru, Steve, 236

Fakir (Dostum lieutenant), 188, 189

Fallujah, 222–29

Fedayeen Saddam, 51, 53, 61, 80,
    116

Fonseca, Luis, Jr., 111–12, 112–13,
    114–22, 122–24, 241
  Nasiriyah, battle at, 112–13
  Navy Cross awarded to, 123–24,
    125–26
  Saddam Canal Bridge, 113,
    114–22, 122

Fowler, Andrew, 44

FOX News, 237

Frank, Barney, 235

Franklin, Thomas "Tank," 24, 25,
    28, 31

Gallegos, Jeremiah, 42

García, Eric, 104

García, Lance Corporal, 58

Gardner, Lance Corporal, 57, 58, 59,
    61–62

General Douglas MacArthur
    Leadership Award, 130

Glass, Randy, 117–18, 120–22, 123

Goldberg, Whoopi, 240
Good Morning America (ABC), 239
Greatest Generation, The (Brokaw), 14
Greco, Richard, 171–72

Hagee, Michael W., 32
Hammond, Captain, 51
Hannity, Sean , 237
Hannity & Colmes (FOX News), 237
Hanson, Victor Davis, 245
Hardball (MSNBC), 237
Harnden, Toby, 238–39
Harris, Dan, 239
Haynes, William, III, 140, 144
    Bronze Star awarded to, 151
Hester, Jerry (father), 152
Hester, Leigh Ann, 140, 142–43, 143–44, 144–51, 236
    and Raven 42, 140–41, 143–44, 144–51
    Silver Star awarded to, 140, 151–52
Hewitt, Hugh, 244
Holbrooke, Master Sergeant, 157
Hollin, Lincoln D., 211
Home of Heros (blog), 244
Hussein, Saddam, 239, 246
Hussein, Uday, 80

Internet bloggers, 146, 243–44

Jaramillo, Corporal, 58
Johnson, Lyndon Baines, 202

Jordan, Eason, 235, 240
Jordan, Patrick, 130, 131
Jukes, Steven, 238
Jumper, John, 72
Juska, Matthew, 101, 102, 103–4, 105, 105–6

Kaemmerer, T. J., 224, 225–28
Keegan, John, 93
Keith, Sergeant, 98
Keller, Matthew, 209, 211
Kelley, Thomas, 14
Kennedy, Mary, 39, 40, 45–46
Keough, Jason, 117–18
Kerman, Robert "Robbie," 21–25, 31–36
    Highway 1, attacked on, 25–31
    Silver Star awarded to, 32
Kilgore, Charles, 42
Korean War, fatalities, 14
Korte, Corporal, 24, 25
Kurtz, Howard, 238

LaBelle, James, 226
Laery, Alex, 213
Lalota, Dan, 170
Leary, Alex, 237
LeHew, Aisley (daughter), 87
LeHew, Cynthia (wife), 87
LeHew, Justin, 13, 87–90, 90–92, 92–107
    Nasiriyah, battle at, 90, 92–106
    Navy Cross awarded to, 89–90, 109–10

Linder, Todd M., 146
Lindh, John Walker, 180, 195, 241
Lynch, Jessica, 89

McCabe, Vick, 158
McCormack, Greg, 70
McCormick, Armand, 21–25, 31–36
  Highway 1, attacked on, 25–31
  politics of, 33–35
  Silver Star awarded to, 32
McCullough, David, 247
Mack, Bryan, 140, 144
McKinney, Cynthia, 245
Mahdi Army, 130, 132
Marine Expeditionary Unit (MEU),
  89
Markham, William "Calvin," 15,
  67–69, 69–70, 70–74
  American flag, rescue of, 73
  and opponents to the war, 74, 243
  reconnaissance mission, 70–73
  Silver Star awarded to, 75–76
Martin, Matt, 102
Martínez, Marco, 15, 49–50, 241
  ambush, responding to, 50–64
  Navy Cross awarded to, 62, 65–66
  and the war in Iraq, 63
Mason, Richard A., 228
Matthews, Chris, 237
Mazar-e-Sharif, 183–84, 187
Mead, Michael, 117–18, 120–22, 123
Medal of Honor, 202–3, 215,
  217–18, 230–31, 234
Medal of Honor (Mikaelian), 202

media
  and the War on Terror, 233–48
Mehdi, Buthana, 246
Meyers, Lacey, 33
Meyers, Tom, 114
Mikaelian, Allen, 202
Mike, Jason, 236
  and Raven 42, 143–44, 144–51
  Silver Star awarded to, 151–52
Miles, Lance Corporal, 98
Mitchell, Bill, 135–36
Mitchell, Mark, 179–180, 181–82,
  182–95, 195–97, 241
  Distinguished Service Cross
    awarded to, 196, 197, 199
  Qala-i-Jangi Fortress uprising, 180
  on the War on Terror, 196–97
Mitchell, Michael, 134–36
Mohammed, 41
Moore, John C., 130, 132, 133
Moore, Michael, 240
Morel, Amy (wife), 173
Morel, Brent L., 165–67, 167–71
  bronze statue of, 165
  Navy Cross awarded to, 171–72,
    175–76
  Al Anbar Province reconnaissance
    mission, 167–71
Morel, Mike (father), 165, 165–66,
  172–73
Morel, Molly (mother), 165–66, 172
Morris, Dustin, 140, 144, 145
  Army Commendation Medal
    awarded to, 151

Morrison, Adam, 227
Moyers, Bill, 240
Mudville Gazette (blog), 244
Murdock, Jacob M., 227
Murphy, Audie, 14

Najaf, 40–44
Nasiriyah, 90, 92–106, 112–13
National Geographic, 235, 236
National Review, 240–41
Navy Cross, 32, 37–38, 62, 65–66,
    89–90, 109–10, 123–24, 125–26,
    166, 171–72, 175–76, 176–77
NBC, 235, 236
Nein, Timothy, 236
    and Raven 42, 143–44, 144–51
    Silver Star awarded to, 151–52
New York Times, 135, 142, 240, 246
    and Abu Ghraib prison abuses,
    234
Newby, Steven, 42
Newsweek, 195
Nimitz, Chester, 14
Northern Alliance, 70–73
Now (PBS), 240

O'Beirne, Kate, 240–41
O'Hare, Carl Brashear Edward
    "Butch," 14
Operation Enduring Freedom,
    245
Operation Iraqi Freedom, 33, 44, 79,
    82
    opposition to, 135–36

Ordunez, Jesse, 140, 144
    Army Commendation Medal
    awarded to, 151

Patton, George, 202
PBS, 240
Peralta, Icela (sister), 230
Peralta, Karen (sister), 221, 230
Peralta, Rafael, 219–20, 220–22,
    222–29, 229–32
    Fallujah, battle of, 222–29
    Medal of Honor nominee,
    230–32
    Purple Heart awarded to, 230
Peralta, Ricardo (brother), 219, 221,
    230
Peralta, Rosa (mother), 220, 230
Pitruzzello, Marilyn, 77, 81
Pitruzzello, Tom, 81
Pizzey, Allen, 239
Pohlmann, William T., 205–7
Providence Journal, 237–38
Pullen, Ashley, 140–41, 144
    Bronze Star awarded to, 151
Puller, Lewis "Chesty," 14
Purple Heart, 230

Qala-i-Jangi Fortress, 180, 183–84,
    241
    prisoner uprising at, 184–95
Quinn, Holly (wife), 81
Quinn, Patrick, 77–78, 78–83
    Silver Star awarded to, 80–82, 85
    on the war in Iraq, 82

Rakes, Jason, 130, 131

Rather, Dan, 238

Reagan, Ronald, 13

Reuters News Service, 238, 242

Rickenbacker, Eddie, 14

Riojas, José D., 44

Rivera, Joseph, 141, 144, 149

Roberts, Mary Louise, 139–40

Rockwell, Paul, 135

Rogers, Rob, 219, 229

Rooney, Andy, 238, 243

Rumsfeld, Donald, 81–82

Russert, Tim, 247

St. Petersburg Times, 212–13, 237

Saddam Canal Bridge, 106, 113,
    114–22, 122

Saddam Hussein International
    Airport, 210

Sadr City, 132

Sanders, Micheaux, 127–28, 128–36,
    136–37, 137

    Silver Star awarded to, 137

Sasser, Edward, 98

Satler, John, 229

Sawyer, Diane, 239

Schoomaker, Peter, 81

Seaman, Michael, 213, 214

September 11 (9/11), 16, 23, 24, 196,
    197, 244–45

Sheehan, Cindy, 135

Sherman, William Tecumseh, 233

Silver Star, 32, 44–45, 75–76, 80–82,
    85, 137, 140, 151–52, 163–64

60 Minutes (CBS News), 238

Small, Adam, 39, 40–44, 241

Smash (blog), 244

Smith, Birgit (wife), 201, 204–5, 208,
    214–15, 216

Smith, David (son), 201, 205, 216

Smith, Jessica (stepdaughter), 201,
    205, 216

Smith, Justin, 97

Smith, Paul Ray, 15, 201–3, 203–9,
    209–16, 237

    battle near Saddam Hussein
        International Airport, 210–14

    Medal of Honor awarded to,
        202–3, 215, 217–18, 230, 234

Smith, Thomas, 209–10

Soldier's Creed, 45, 47

Sonntag, Kurt, 185–86

Spann, Johnny "Mike," 179, 184,
    194–95, 241

Spann, Shannon (wife), 179–80

Special Forces (SF), 181–82

Spectator, 238–39

Streisand, Barbara, 240

Sullivan, Helen, 81

Sunday Morning (CBS), 239

Taliban fighters, 67, 70–73, 161,
    180

    Qala-i-Jangi Fortress uprising,
        184–95

Talkington, Rory, 171

Tardif, Timothy C., 52, 55–56, 61–62

Tenet, George, 194

Tenth Special Forces Group (SFG), 78–79

Terry, Stan, 77–78, 82–83

Thompson, James, 91

Thompson, Sergeant, 101–2, 104–5

Truman, Harry S., 202

Tuggle, Major, 103, 105

Turner, Ted, 237–38

U.S. Army Special Forces Command (USASFC), 78–79

Velásquez, Alex, 99, 101, 102, 104

Vietnam War, fatalities, 14

Vines, John R., 139, 151

War on Terror, 16, 17–18, 196–97
    mainstream media and, 233–48

Washington, George, 247

Washington Post, 144, 236, 238

"White Lightning," 160

women
    role in the U.S. military, 142

Woolsey, Jim, 112

World War I, fatalities, 14

World War II, 14–15
    fatalities, 14

Wright, Eddie, 168

Yetter, Kevin, 212, 213